Maxwell E. Johnson

Images
of Baptism

LTP

**Liturgy Training Publications
in cooperation with**

**The North American Forum
on the Catechumenate**

Acknowledgments

The *Forum Essay* series is a cooperative effort of The North American Forum on the Catechumenate and Liturgy Training Publications. The purpose of this series is to provide a forum for exploring issues emerging from the implementation of the order of Christian initiation and from the renewal of the practice of reconciliation in the Roman Catholic Church.

Otdher titles in the series:

The Role of the Assembly in Christian Initiation
 Catherine Vincie, RSHM
Eucharist as Sacrament of Initiation
 Nathan D. Mitchell
On the Rite of Election
 Rita Ferrone
Preaching the Rites of Christian Initiation
 Jan Michael Joncas
Liturgical Spirituality and the Rite of Christian Initiation of Adults
 Shawn Madigan

IMAGES OF BAPTISM © 2001 Archdiocese of Chicago: Liturgy Training Publications, 1800 North Hermitage Avenue, Chicago IL 60622-1101; 1-800-933-1800, fax 1-800-933-7094, e-mail orders@ltp.org. All rights reserved. See our website at www.ltp.org.

All scripture citations are taken from the *New Revised Standard Version* Bible, © 1989, Division of Christian Education of the National Council of Churches of Christ in the United States of America.

All citations of liturgical texts from E. C. Whitaker, *Documents of the Baptismal Liturgy* (London: SPCK, 1970) appear courtesy of SPCK.

The text of "The Church of Christ in Every Age," page 29, by Fred Pratt Green 1971 © Hope Publishing Company is used with permission. All rights reserved.

This *Forum Essay* was designed by Mary Bowers and typeset in Frutiger and Bembo by Jim Mellody-Pizzato. The cover design is by Barb Rohm. Theresa Pincich was the production editor. Printed by Printing Arts Chicago in Cicero, Illinois. Editors for the series are Victoria M. Tufano (Liturgy Training Publications) and Jim Schellman (The North American Forum on the Catechumenate).

Library of Congress Catalog Card Number: 2001086934

1-56854-321-2
IMGBAP
05　04　03　02　01　　　5　4　3　2　1

Contents

■

Introduction

In his *Procatechesis,* an introductory lecture to the "elect" or *photizomenoi* (i.e., "those to be enlightened") at the start of their lenten journey to Easter baptism, the late-fourth-century bishop Cyril (or John) of Jerusalem describes the meaning of baptism by means of several rich images and metaphors:

> Great indeed is the baptism which is offered you. It is a ransom to captives; the remission of offences; the death of sin; the regeneration of the soul; the garment of light; the holy seal indissoluble; the chariot to heaven; the luxury of paradise; a procuring of the kingdom; the gift of adoption.[1]

Although Cyril's own primary interpretative image for baptism would undoubtedly be the death, burial and resurrection of the baptized in Christ (Romans 6)—an interpretation curiously absent from the above "definition"—his assortment of images in the *Procatechesis* is highly consistent with the rich variety and diversity of baptismal images provided within the New Testament itself.

For, like Cyril in this passage, the New Testament does not present us with an authoritative definition or single image by which the church interpreted the meaning and implications of baptism. Instead, it is clear from the New Testament that the meaning of baptism was understood by means of several diverse, albeit complementary, images. In other words, according to the New Testament, baptism is forgiveness of sins and the gift of the Holy Spirit (Acts 2:38); new birth through water and the Holy Spirit (John 3:5; Titus 3:5–7); putting off of the "old nature" and "putting on the new," that is, "being clothed in the righteousness of Christ" (Galatians 3:27; Colossians 3:9–10); initiation into the "one body" of the Christian community (1 Corinthians 12:13; see also Acts 2:42); washing, sanctification and justification in Christ and the Holy Spirit (1 Corinthians 6:11); enlightenment (Hebrews 6:4; 10:32; 1 Peter 2:9); being "anointed" and/or "sealed" by the Holy Spirit (2 Corinthians 1:21–22; 1 John 2:20, 27); being "sealed" or "marked" as belonging to God and God's people (2 Corinthians 1:21–22; Ephesians 1:13–14; 4:30, Revelation 7:3); and, of course, being joined to Christ through participation in his death, burial and resurrection (Romans 6:3–11; Colossians 2:12–15).

Anglican liturgiologist Paul Bradshaw has noted that "this variation in baptismal theology encourages the supposition that the ritual itself may also have varied considerably from place to place" in the earliest period of the church.[2] And if they were not present in some places at that time, these baptismal images give rise to specific ritual practices later on. Anointings with oil, for example, will develop in all early Christian liturgical traditions to express ritually the gift, anointing and seal of the Holy Spirit in baptism. Putting off the old nature and being clothed with the new nature of Christ (Galatians 3:27) will eventually be expressed by the prebaptismal stripping of clothes and the postbaptismal clothing in new white garments. The mark of God's ownership of the newly baptized will come to be signified by various signings or consignations with the cross, either connected to an anointing or not. Enlightenment will be expressed by the use of baptismal candles or tapers. And the baptismal font and waters will come to be interpreted as either or both womb (John 3:5) and tomb (Romans 6), grave and mother. Given the variety of New Testament interpretations of baptism, it was inevitable that the rites themselves would evolve in this way. Rich biblical imagery such as this would seem to call for an equally rich liturgical expression and practice.

If in our own day, thanks in large part to the post–Vatican II restoration of the catechumenate and Easter baptism in the Roman Catholic *Rite of Christian Initiation of Adults* (RCIA), and similar restorations under way in other liturgical traditions, the image of Romans 6 has become again the dominant interpretative metaphor for baptism in the contemporary church, the baptismal liturgies themselves actually preserve a number of other images. Note, for example, the symphony of baptismal images in the prayer for the blessing of water at the Easter Vigil in the Roman Rite:

> Father,
> you give us grace through sacramental signs,
> which tell us of the wonders of your unseen power.
>
> In baptism we use your gift of water,
> which you have made a rich symbol of the grace
> you give us in this sacrament.
>
> At the very dawn of creation
> your Spirit breathed on the waters,
> making them the wellspring of all holiness.
>
> The waters of the great flood
> you made a sign of the waters of baptism
> that make an end of sin
> and a new beginning of goodness.
>
> Through the waters of the Red Sea
> you led Israel out of slavery

to be an image of God's holy people,
set free from sin by baptism.

In the waters of the Jordan
your Son was baptized by John
and anointed with the Spirit.

Your Son willed that water and blood should flow from his side
as he hung upon the cross.

After his resurrection he told his disciples:
"Go out and teach all nations,
baptizing them in the name of the Father, and of the Son,
and of the Holy Spirit."

Father,
look now with love upon your Church
and unseal for it the fountain of baptism.

By the power of the Holy Spirit
give to this water the grace of your Son,
so that in the sacrament of baptism
all those whom you have created in your likeness
may be cleansed from sin
and rise to a new birth of innocence
by water and the Holy Spirit.

We ask you Father, with your Son
to send the Holy Spirit upon the waters of this font.

May all who are buried with Christ in the death of baptism
rise also with him to newness of life.

We ask this through Christ our Lord.
Amen.[3]

Similarly, the significant 1982 ecumenical convergence statement produced by the Faith and Order Commission of the World Council of Churches, *Baptism, Eucharist, Ministry* (BEM), invites us to recover the rich multi-dimensional imagery of baptism in our common liturgical tradition by treating the meaning of baptism under the categories of "Participation in Christ's Death and Resurrection," "Conversion, Pardoning and Cleansing," "The Gift of the Spirit," "Incorporation into the Body of Christ" and "The Sign of the Kingdom."[4] By way of introduction to these images, BEM states:

Baptism is the sign of new life through Jesus Christ. It unites the one baptized with Christ and with his people. The New Testament scriptures and the liturgy of the Church unfold the meaning of baptism in various images which express the riches of Christ and the gifts of his salvation. These images are sometimes linked with the symbolic uses of water in the Old Testament. Baptism is participation in Christ's death and resurrection (Romans 6:3–5; Colossians 2:12); a washing away of sin (1 Corinthians 6:11); a new birth (John 3:5); an enlightenment by Christ (Ephesians 5:14); a re-clothing in Christ (Galatians 3:27); a renewal by the Spirit (Titus 3:5); the experience of salvation from the flood (1 Peter 3:20–21); an exodus from bondage (1 Corinthians 10:1–2) and a liberation into a new humanity in which barriers of division whether or sex or race or social status are transcended (Galatians 3:27–28; 1 Corinthians 12:13). The images are many but the reality is one.[5]

"The images are many but the reality is one." This short book on baptismal imagery has been written to offer primarily catechists, parish liturgists, pastors, religious educators and, indeed, all who are involved in the church's baptismal ministries, with a study of some of the key baptismal images and metaphors that scripture and the church's great liturgical traditions hand on to us in an attempt toward recovering those images for the church today. As such, these images provide for us models by which we might glimpse some of the manifold riches that baptism is and offers to us. Hence, we might say that it is precisely a variety of models for conceptualizing, catechizing and celebrating baptism that these images provide. However, because any model is itself limited to features that fit the model and must suppress features that don't fit, none of these images should be taken individually in any kind of comprehensive way as the *only* way to envision baptism, although a case could surely be made that in our history we have often allowed some baptismal models (e.g., baptism as liberation from original sin or as death and resurrection) to function in such an exclusive manner. It is precisely because any given model does

not present the whole picture of a particular phenomenon that a model can become a useful tool in illuminating significant aspects of the entire, in this case, baptismal
process, which another model might necessarily suppress.
Hence, like symbols themselves, models are most useful
because they give rise to thought and invite further
reflection.[6] This book is about the thought and reflection that these images invite.

Several years ago, in an address I gave in Minneapolis,
Minnesota, to the Roman Catholic Federation of
Diocesan Liturgical Commissions at their annual meet-
ing, I made the following statement:

> For good theological reasons we have centered our attention
> on the connection between Easter, especially the Easter Vigil,
> and Christian initiation. But even if centered here, the bap-
> tismal tradition of the church is much richer than this. Over
> the past twenty years or so, contemporary liturgical scholar-
> ship has helped us understand that while there was an early
> *preference* for initiation at Easter in the churches of North
> Africa and Rome, other churches—e.g., those of Syria, Egypt,
> and the non-Roman Western churches in Gaul and Spain—
> tended to focus on other occasions like Epiphany, understood,
> of course, as the great theophany of Christ in the Jordan, and
> that a Romans 6 (death/resurrection) theology of baptism
> came to the forefront of sacramental theology universally only
> within a fourth-century post-Nicene context. Prior to that,
> the dominant interpretation and paradigm of initiation appears
> to have been that of Jesus' own baptism in the Jordan and the
> rebirth imagery of John 3. And from such a focus in this
> equally ancient and biblical tradition comes a whole cluster
> of initiation images that have little to do with passing from
> death to life, or with sharing in the dying and rising of Christ
> through baptism. Such images, extremely suggestive in the
> case of infants, include seeing the font as *womb* rather than
> tomb, literally called the "Jordan" itself in some traditions,
> images like "adoption, divinization, sanctification, gift of the
> Spirit, indwelling, glory, power, wisdom, rebirth, restoration,
> [and] mission." Other feasts, then, such as Epiphany, the
> Baptism of our Lord, Pentecost, All Saints, or the annual feast
> of the parish patron saint, all of which could be preceded by
> some adaptation of the catechumenal process for the parents

and sponsors of infants and all of which could receive their own baptismal vigil, would be ideal occasions for such common celebrations. We have clearly recovered the baptismal focus of Lent and Easter. Why not, for example, Advent as well? Initiation into Christ is more than participation in his death and resurrection. And we would do well in our catechesis and celebration throughout the year to recover and re-emphasize this diversity of images.[7]

In response to this statement, Vicky Tufano from Liturgy Training Publications, and Thom Morris, then executive director of the North American Forum on the Catechumenate, approached me with a gracious invitation to consider writing a book that would aid in such a recovery and re-emphasis on this diversity of baptismal images for the *Forum Essays* series published by Liturgy Training Publications. This book is the result of that conversation and invitation.

It should be noted from the beginning that not all possible New Testament baptismal images or models are treated herein. Out of the several that could be studied, only those which have suggested themselves as dominant or primary in the evolution of the Christian liturgical tradition, and only those that have some obvious correlation to the major solemnities, feasts and seasons of the liturgical year have been selected. Here I have been influenced decisively by the rubric in the *Book of Common Prayer* of the Episcopal Church, USA, which directs that

> Holy Baptism is especially appropriate at the Easter Vigil, on the Day of Pentecost, on All Saints' Day or the Sunday after All Saints' Day, [and] on the Feast of the Baptism of our Lord (the first Sunday after the Epiphany). It is recommended that, as far as possible, Baptisms be reserved for these occasions or when a bishop is present.[8]

Consequently, I have chosen only four baptismal images or metaphors for the chapters of this study: Chapter 1: Baptism as Participation in the Death, Burial, and Resurrection of Christ; Chapter 2: Baptism as New Birth or Adoption by Water and the Holy Spirit; Chapter

3: Baptism as the Sacrament and Seal of the Holy Spirit; and Chapter 4: Baptism as Initiation or Incorporation into Christ and the Church. Although my method throughout, as will be seen, is strongly rooted in the historical study of liturgy, this book is generally much more pastoral, catechetical, or even, I suppose, mystagogical in orientation than merely providing an historical or theological analysis of liturgical rites and texts. Nevertheless, Chapters 1 and 2 provide an historical-theological introduction to the individual image in question, and each chapter does contain several historical, theological and liturgical texts that can assist in our recovery of these images today. I do not shy away from making either critical judgments or prescriptive statements about how the recovery of such images or models might, in my opinion, best be allowed to function within the various liturgical traditions of the churches today, even if that might mean, ultimately, certain changes beyond the authority of the pastoral liturgist at this time in history.

Reference to "the various liturgical traditions of the church*es*" in the previous sentence is deliberate. This book is written not only from a decidedly ecumenical perspective but also, it is hoped, for an ecumenical audience, at the very least for Roman Catholics, Episcopalians and Lutherans, who hold so much of the Western liturgical tradition in common and who will find much of their own rites and theologies reflected in the text. To that end, liturgical texts, sources, and authors from both East and West—Eastern Christian (at least from the Patristic period), Roman Catholic and various Protestant traditions—are included. Of all the sacraments, treating baptism with an ecumenical approach surely needs no defense today. In spite of various church-dividing differences that remain as ecumenical challenges in the common pursuit of full and visible communion among the churches, the centrality of baptism in the life of the church and the contemporary ecumenical convergence in baptismal theology and liturgical practice serve to remind us strongly that all Christian life, identity and vocation flows from our common baptismal plunge into the waters of the font with Christ, where in the words of the introduction to "Holy Baptism" in the *Lutheran Book of Worship*

> . . . our gracious heavenly Father liberates us from sin and death by joining us to the death and resurrection of our Lord Jesus Christ. We are born children of a fallen humanity; in the waters of Baptism we are reborn children of God and inheritors of eternal life. By water and the Holy Spirit we are made members of the Church which is the body of Christ. As we live with him and with his people, we grow in faith, love and obedience to the will of God.[9]

Finally, I wish to acknowledge those who have contributed in whatever way to the completion of this book. First, special thanks goes to my graduate assistant, David Maxwell, for his assistance in research and careful proofreading of the manuscript. Second, I wish to thank Sister Eleanor Bernstein, CSJ, director of the Notre Dame Center for Pastoral Liturgy, for her most helpful comments and suggestions throughout the research and writing process, as well as her making available to me several resources from the Center. Third, my appreciation goes to Father Joseph Weiss, SJ, associate director of the Notre Dame Center for Pastoral Liturgy, for his critique, comments and suggestions. And, of course, my thanks go finally also to Vicky Tufano, who first suggested the book, and for her patience and care in guiding it to completion.

Chapter 1

Baptism as Participation in the Death, Burial and Resurrection of Christ

■

> Do you not know that all of us who have been baptized in
> Christ Jesus were baptized into his death? Therefore we have
> been buried with him by baptism into death, so that, just as
> Christ was raised from the dead by the glory of the Father, we
> too might walk in newness of life. For if we have been united
> with him in a death like his, we will certainly be united with
> him in a resurrection like his. We know that our old self was
> crucified with him so that the body of sin might be destroyed,
> and we might no longer be enslaved to sin. For whoever has
> died is freed from sin. But if we have died with Christ, we
> believe that we will also live with him. We know that Christ,
> being raised from the dead, will never die again; death no
> longer has dominion over him. The death he died, he died to
> sin, once for all; but the life he lives, he lives to God. So you
> also must consider yourselves dead to sin and alive to God in
> Christ Jesus. (Romans 6:3–11)

Of all the possible biblical and liturgical images of baptism, certainly the understanding that baptism sacramentally signifies and effects our participation in the death, burial and resurrection of Christ is, in our day and age, the most readily available and dominant one. Thanks especially to the Roman Catholic restoration of the Paschal Triduum and the concomitant restoration of the adult catechumenate and Easter baptism in the *Rite of Christian Initiation of Adults,* as well as in the revised liturgical books of several other Christian traditions today,

1

what we have come to call the "Paschal Mystery," the great mystery of Christ's death and resurrection, has emerged as the key image and central metaphor by which all Christian life and liturgy are to be interpreted and understood. Within almost all of our churches in recent years, Easter and its Triduum have achieved their rightful place as the very center of the liturgical year. After a Lent of penitential return to our origins in the font, we initiate new members of Christ's body and we renew and reaffirm our plunge into the mystery of Christ's death and resurrection as both our sacramental passage through him with him and in him from death to life and as the cruciform pattern or model of our common postbaptismal life as his body in the world.

The Norm of Easter Baptism?

Because this Paschal Mystery imagery is so common today, it is surprising for us to learn that, apart from some notable exceptions, Easter and baptism in the first few centuries of Christianity probably did not form the kind of integral synthesis that we often imagine that they did or that they do in the contemporary church. In the first three centuries, in fact, we really have only two statements that clearly indicate a connection between them.

The first is that of the North African convert Tertullian, who in his treatise on baptism wrote of his preference for Easter baptism:

> The Passover [i.e., Easter] provides the day of most solemnity for baptism, for then was accomplished our Lord's passion, and *into it we are baptized*. . . . After that, Pentecost is a most auspicious period for arranging baptisms, for during it our Lord's resurrection was several times made known among the disciples, and the grace of the Holy Spirit first given. . . . For all that, every day is a Lord's day: any hour, any season, is suitable for baptism. If there is any difference of solemnity, it makes no difference to the grace.[1]

Unfortunately, we have no way of knowing whether Tertullian was reflecting the actual practice of the North African church of his day or merely advocating a personal preference. In fact, his references to "Pentecost," most likely the fifty days of what we now call the Easter Season, and to "any hour, any season" as "suitable for baptism" surely suggest that he himself knew a variety of baptismal occasions within North African Christianity.

That baptisms did take place on Easter in the Roman church of the early third century is certainly witnessed to by Hippolytus of Rome, not in the so-called *Apostolic Tradition,* which is often attributed to him and makes *no* reference to Easter baptism whatsoever, but in his *Commentary on Daniel* (13:15):

> On that day [the Pasch] the bath is prepared in the Garden for those who are burning and the church . . . is presented to God as a pure bride; and faith and charity, like [Susanna's] companions, prepare the oil and the unguents for those being washed. What are the unguents but the commandments of the Word? What is the oil but the power of the Holy Spirit, with which, like perfume, believers are anointed after the bath?[2]

But even here we have no way of knowing whether baptisms did or did not take place on other occasions as well in the Roman church of the early third century.

Apart from these references, hard evidence for Easter baptism in the first few centuries of the church does not exist, and Easter itself appears not to have been interpreted originally as either the passage of Christ from death to life or as the Christian's passage from death to life through baptism with him. Rather, as modern scholarship on the liturgical year has argued, the annual Easter, or Pascha feast, probably celebrated, as in Quartodeciman practice, on the 14th day of the Jewish month Nisan (the annual date of Passover, which became either March 25 or April 6 in various adaptations of the Julian calendar), took its meaning from an interpretation of *Pascha* as *paschein,* meaning "to suffer."[3] Hence, as Raniero Cantalamessa has argued, Pascha was about the suffering, or "passion," of Christ, who alone was the protagonist of the feast, which even in a pre-Nicene context commemorated primarily his death as the Paschal Lamb on the historical date associated with his Passion. Only later, and thanks in large part to the Alexandrian theological tradition, as reflected in the writings of the great theologian and biblical exegete Origen, did Pascha begin to be interpreted as "passage" and, consequently and logically, will begin to attract the celebration of baptism to itself.[4]

At the same time, it is important to note that, while Origen himself made frequent reference to Romans 6 in his writings, the Alexandrian tradition itself appears not to have known Easter baptism either in Origen's time or in subsequent centuries. Even today in the Coptic Orthodox church, the rubric remains that baptisms are not to take place between Palm Sunday and Pentecost.[5] The clear and almost universal connection of Easter and baptism, then, seems to have been part of what has been called the "post-Nicene synthesis," where in the aftermath of the Council of Nicea (AD 325), not only does Easter baptism with a concomitant rediscovery or reappropriation of Romans 6 theology begin to show up almost everywhere in the church, both East and West, but also the season of Lent as a "forty-day" period of preparation for both baptism and Easter similarly makes its universal appearance. Easter baptism, viewed through the lens of Romans 6, although already at least an emerging *preference* in the West (Tertullian and Hippolytus), probably becomes, for a variety of reasons,[6] the universal Christian *ideal* for baptism and its interpretation only in the late fourth century. By the time of Augustine of Hippo, the synthesis of Easter as "passage" and Easter baptism as part of that passage is certainly complete.[7] That it had already moved strongly in this direction in the late fourth century Christian East is witnessed to in the catechetical lectures of bishops like Cyril of Jerusalem

4

and John Chrysostom; in the non-Roman West it is indicated in the catechetical lectures of Augustine's own baptizer, Ambrose of Milan. In the baptismal theology of all of these great mystagogues certainly Romans 6 is the dominant, if not the only, baptismal image they favor. But, as Paul Bradshaw, in a compelling essay on the development of baptism at Easter, as well as at other feasts in Christian antiquity, has concluded

> [w]hatever the *theory* may have been in some places . . . it looks as though baptism at Easter was never the normative *practice* in Christian antiquity that many have assumed. The most that can be said is that it was an experiment that survived for less than fifty years. Like the seed sown on rocky ground, it endured for a while but eventually withered away.[8]

For whatever reason St. Paul's Romans 6 theology of baptism remained strangely silent in the first few centuries of the church's existence, the following reasons certainly underscore the importance of this image and the need for our extended reflection: (1) the reappropriation of baptism as death, burial and resurrection in Christ by the late-fourth-century church; (2) the preservation of what, in Bradshaw's words, became the theoretical *norm* or *ideal* of Easter baptism in the liturgical books of almost all Christian traditions throughout the ages; and (3) the modern restoration and recovery of Easter baptism in theory and practice for the churches today. How, then, might this foundational and rich image or metaphor of baptismal death, burial and resurrection in Christ be rescued from the realm of contemporary cliché and brought to new life within the church today? It is to this question that this chapter is devoted.

Letting Death Be Death

Death and burial (at least in large areas of the United States) are not what they used to be. There was a time when people usually died in their homes surrounded by immediate family, extended family and other loved ones; when they were lovingly prepared for burial by their families; and when, after the funeral, they were buried with the full, active and conscious participation and assistance of the gathered assembly itself, often in a cemetery adjacent to the church building. Today, with the notable exception of hospice programs and deliberate pastoral-liturgical attempts to reintegrate literal burial into the funeral rites, death has been gradually divorced from life and given over to modern medical technology as well as, ultimately, to those in the funeral industry. Even the funeral services themselves frequently take place in funeral "homes" or "chapels" that are devoid of recognizable and common Christian symbols, rather than in churches where the deceased worshiped. Many in our contemporary world share Etty Hillesum's experience of living in a culture where one almost never encounters death until it becomes personal:

> It sounds paradoxical: By excluding death from our life we cannot live a full life, and by admitting death into our life we enlarge and enrich it. This has been my first real confrontation with death. I never knew what to make of it before. I had such a virginal attitude towards it. I have never seen a dead person. Just imagine: A world sown with a million corpses, and in twenty-seven years I have never seen a single one. I have often wondered what my attitude to death really is. I never delved deeply into the question: There was no need for that. And now death has come as large as life and I greet him as an old acquaintance. Everything is so simple. You don't have to have any profound thoughts on the subject. There death suddenly stands, large as life and part of it.[9]

Whether our contemporary culture is truly a "culture of death" any more than any other, or whether, like all cultures past and present, ours is also involved, sometimes quietly, sometimes violently, in a restless quest toward and a disordered pursuit of the fullness of life and ultimate meaning ("Our hearts are restless until they come to rest in you, O God" to paraphrase St. Augustine's classic prayer), one thing (beyond death itself, of course) appears to be certain. That is, as in the title of Ernst Becker's best-selling 1973 book, *The Denial of Death,* we are, it seems, a culture bent on denying death, on shielding death from ourselves, of ignoring its bitter reality until we can ignore it no more. But, even then, we continue to deny it through our practices of embalming and our cosmetic and often illusory attempts at bodily restoration. As the late Lutheran theologian Joseph Sittler put it:

> Professor Hans Jonas once wrote an essay in which he mused over the disposition of our generation to regard death as an awkward interruption of a play that was so pleasantly getting on very well. Human life has been increasingly brought under such managerial powers as to make death a cheat, a ludicrous interruption, an event for which an entire profession has conspired to cosmetize the dead and narcotize the survivors.[10]

The first step in our appropriation of the image of baptism as participation in the death, burial and resurrection of Christ today, then, must surely be to let death be death. Jennifer (Sr. Genevieve) Glen calls precisely, if indirectly, for such an honest approach to the phenomenon of death:

> Whether [sickness] befalls us suddenly or develops slowly, whether it turns out to be minor or chronic or terminal, it seems always to take us by surprise. We know intellectually that we are ultimately finite, but we seem unprepared for the limits beyond which our bodily being will not take us. Illness, therefore, deprives us of our projected future. In so doing, particularly if it is serious, it threatens the destruction of faith and hope. We have placed the most basic of unspoken trusts in our bodily life, and it has betrayed us. Because of that betrayal we can no longer place any real trust in the future. Hope requires that we project that future as both possible and desirable. To the person who is seriously ill, the future often seems to be neither. Time shrinks to the eternal now, beyond which "be dragons" — in the words of the ancient cartographers labeling the unknown edges of the world. Beyond lies the

ultimate betrayal which is death, now recognized as certain even if not immediate. The vision of death lurking within the experience of sickness seems to cut off the future absolutely, at least from the experiential and imaginative viewpoint. With the loss of the future goes the loss of meaning. That toward which life was lived, however unreflectively, no longer gives purpose and direction to the many relationships which constitute our world. In the face of the insuperable barrier of death, concealed behind the immediate limit of present sickness, life and its relationships threaten to become absurd. . . . [Confronted with the inescapable prospect of my own death,] if not now then surely one day, my world has shattered into pieces at my feet. I never expected this, and now I do not know what to do. I suppose I should do something about it, about my person, about my loved ones, about my religion—but to tell you the truth, I don't know if I want to bother. What is the use? None of it makes any sense anymore anyway. The future is gone, meaning is gone. All the relationships which defined me—intrapersonal, interpersonal and transpersonal—are in shambles. Heal that, if you will![11]

But if we are to let our own deaths *be* death then so too must we let the death of *Christ* on the cross also be a real *death* before moving so quickly to his resurrection, which, after all, brings new life not in spite of but *out* of death. For the cross and death of Christ were not merely stages to be endured in some great redemptive religious drama or as part of a religious-cultic act of priestly and sacrifical atonement that Jesus himself, fully knowing already by divine omniscience the outcome of resurrection, merely "passed through" or passively tolerated on the way to reclaiming his former status and glory. Rather, as Swiss-Reformed theologian Jürgen Moltmann has reminded us strongly:

The symbol of the cross in the church points to the God who was crucified not between two candles on an altar but between two thieves in the place of the skull, where the outcasts belong, outside the gates of the city. It is a symbol which therefore leads out of the church and out of religious longing into the fellowship of the oppressed and abandoned.[12]

And, because of this, as he writes elsewhere:

> [The cross] is often better recognized by non-Christians and atheists than by religious Christians because it astonishes and offends them. They see the profrane horror and godlessness of the cross because they do not believe the religious interpretations which have given a meaning to the senselessness of this death. All they find in it is "the image of irreconcilability." To restore Good Friday in all its horror and godlessness (Hegel) it is necessary for Christian faith first of all to abandon the traditional theories of salvation which have made the way the cross is spoken of in Christianity a mere habit. From the very first the Christian faith was distinguished from the religions which surrounded it by its worship of the crucified Christ.[13]

To appropriate the paschal imagery of Romans 6 in our baptismal practice, theology and catechesis we must let death be death, both our own deaths and the death of Christ himself! When St. Paul writes in Romans 6:5 that "we have been united with him in a death like his" or in Galatians 2:19 that he has "been crucified with Christ," he is not simply referring to a ritual act but to the real historical death of Christ by crucifixion, a process of public rejection, humiliation and death he knew all too well in the Roman world of the first century. And, if we are baptized into the death and burial of *Christ,* then we are baptized into *that* death, a death marked at least in the Synoptic Gospel tradition by Jesus' own cry of forsakenness and abandonment: "My God, my God, why have you forsaken me?" (Mark 15:34).

Death in the Christian Liturgical Traditions

Only in letting death be death—both Christ's death and our own—can baptism as participation in the death, burial and resurrection of Christ proclaim a profound and liberating word of new life and hope. Since the late fourth century, at least, this word has been spoken to us **9** and for us time and again, not so much in the liturgical-baptismal texts of our traditions but in the catechetical-theological reflections on baptism by some of the great figures in those traditions. Some of those powerful texts, presented here with little additional comment, may serve us well in our appropriation of and catechesis on this key image today.

Patristic Texts   As already noted, a theological emphasis on Romans 6 as the preferred interpretative image for baptism was certainly a hallmark of the late fourth-century church. The following catechetical-rubrical texts illustrate both the popularity and appeal of this image in that formative historical context.

> Then you were conducted by the hand to the holy pool of sacred baptism, just as Christ was conveyed from the cross to the sepulchre which stands before us. Each person was asked if he believed in the name of the Father and of the Son and of the Holy Spirit. You made the confession that brings salvation, and submerged yourselves three times in the water and emerged: by this symbolic gesture you were secretly re-enacting the burial of Christ three days in the tomb. . . . In one and the same action you died and were born; the water of salvation became both tomb and mother for you. . . . A single moment achieves both ends, and your begetting was simultaneous with your death. . . . What a strange and astonishing situation! We did not really die, we were not really buried, we did not really hang from a cross. Our imitation was symbolic, but our salvation a reality. Christ truly hung from a cross, was truly buried, and truly rose again. All this he did gratuitously for us, that we might share his sufferings by imitating them, and gain salvation in actuality. What transcendent kindness! Christ endured nails in his innocent hands and feet, and suffered pain; and by letting me participate in the pain without anguish or sweat, he freely bestows salvation on me. (Cyril of Jerusalem, *Mystagogical Catechesis* 2. 4–5; circa 387)[14]

> Now concerning baptism, O bishop, or presbyter . . . first anoint the person with holy oil, and afterward baptize him with water, and finally seal him with chrism; that the anointing

with oil may be a participation of the Holy Spirit, *and the water a symbol of the death,* and the chrism a seal of the covenants. . . . But before baptism, let him that is to be baptized fast. (*Apostolic Constitutions,* Book 7:22; circa 381, Syria)[15]

As you know, *baptism is a burial and a resurrection: the old self is buried with Christ to sin and the new nature rises from the dead* "which is being renewed after the image of its creator." We are stripped and we are clothed, stripped of the old garment which has been soiled by the multitude of our sins, clothed with the new that is free from all stain. What does this mean? We are clothed in Christ himself. St. Paul remarks: "As many of you as were baptized into Christ have put on Christ." (John Chrysostom, *Baptismal Homily* II:11; circa 390, Antioch)[16]

So the apostle exclaims, as you have just heard in the reading, "Whoever is baptized, is baptized in the death of Jesus." What does "in the death" mean? It means that just as Christ died, so you will taste death; that just as Christ died to sin and lives to God, so through the sacrament of baptism you are dead to the old enticements of sin and have risen again through the grace of Christ. This is a death, then, not in the reality of bodily death, but in likeness. When you are immersed, you receive the likeness of death and burial, you receive the sacrament of his cross; because Christ hung upon the cross and his body was fastened to it by the nails. So you are crucified with him, you are fastened to Christ, you are fastened by the nails of our Lord Jesus Christ lest the devil pull you away. May Christ's nail continue to hold you, for human weakness seeks to pull you away. (Ambrose of Milan, *De Sacramentis* II.23, circa 391, Milan)[17]

Medieval and Reformation Era Texts As we shall see in more detail in the following chapter, in spite of Easter baptism remaining at least the theoretical norm and ideal in the liturgical books of various traditions from the patristic period on, there are relatively few references to this particular image in the sources themselves from the Western medieval period. For example, the *Gelasian Sacramentary* (late sixth or early seventh century), one of the key documents in the history of the Roman liturgy, merely alludes to this image in its baptismal materials for

Lent and Easter. In the context of the *redditio symboli* (the solemn "return" of the Creed by the elect), after referring to the completion of Christ's resurrection in the baptized, the text states that "in [baptism] is celebrated a kind of death and resurrection," without being more specific.[18]

Outside Rome, in that Western medieval Spanish tradition known as "Mozarabic," extant liturgical and other texts *do* make some reference to this image, though it is by no means the dominant or central one. Hildephonsus of Toledo (+669), in his treatise *De Cognitione Baptismi,* defends the unique Spanish custom of only *one* baptismal immersion:

> That he is once immersed, he is sprinkled in the name of the one Deity. But if he were thrice immersed, the number of the three days of the Lord's burial is shown forth. And therefore within the limits of our faith differing customs are not opposed to one another.[19]

Similarly, an introductory prayer in the eleventh-century Spanish *Liber Ordinum* contains the following statement:

> Dearly beloved, . . . let us join in humble prayer and beseech God . . . : that he may speedily turn hence the approach of evil thoughts and pour his Holy Spirit upon the life-giving water: so that when his people that thirst after faith enter the saving water they may truly be *born again,* as it is written, *of water and the Holy Ghost* [John 3.5], and, being buried in the laver unto their Redeemer, in the manner of a holy and reverend mystery, they may die with him in their baptism and rise again into his kingdom. Amen.[20]

And, of course, in his *Summa Theologiae,* Thomas Aquinas also refers to Romans 6 but it is usually in such a way as merely to underscore the importance of baptism by immersion rather than by some other, equally valid, form. So, for example, Thomas writes:

> Moreover, St Paul says, *Do you not know that all of us who have been baptized into Christ Jesus were baptized into his death? We were buried therefore with him by baptism into death.* But this happens

in immersion, for Chrysostom says on John, *Unless one is born of water and the Holy Spirit,* etc. *When we submerge our heads in the water, so entering into a tomb of sorts, the old man is buried, and, submerged in the depths, he is hidden from view; from there he rises again a new man.*[21]

Elsewhere, he continues:

The symbolism of the burial of Christ is more expressly represented in immersion and thus this manner of baptizing is more common and more praiseworthy. But it is also represented in some fashion in the other ways of baptizing, even though not so clearly. For in whatever way the washing is done, a man's body or some part of it is put under water, just as the body of Christ was placed under the earth.[22]

The relatively few references to Romans 6 in the Western medieval period need not be taken, of course, as indicating that baptism as death, burial and resurrection in Christ was somehow absent from medieval theology. In fact, the rubrical directives in the official liturgical books for Easter baptism at least provided the celebration of baptism with this sort of overall hermeneutic-interpretative context. Even when the infants of Christian parents began to replace adults as the primary candidates for baptism in the early medieval period, at least according to the *Gelasian Sacramentary* and some other sources, it should be noted that parents were still expected and directed to enroll their infants in the Lenten catechumenate and bring them to the three or, later, seven prebaptismal scrutinies in preparation for Easter baptism.[23] Nevertheless, such remnants of the former full lenten catechumenate and Easter baptism tended to be short-lived. Thanks, undoubtedly, to the Augustinian legacy of the doctrine of original sin, together with high rates of infant mortality and the increasing practice—and various diocesan legislation in support—of baptism *quamprimum* ("as soon as possible after birth"), the connection of baptism with Easter and, consequently with this image, tended to be lost in any kind of direct manner. That is, if the rites tended not to use this image to any great extent and if the connection to this image was primarily contextual in terms of Easter baptism itself, then the lack of Easter baptism, with the notable exception of those infants born in close proximity to Easter in a given year, may well have influenced the removal of this image from baptismal consciousness. At the same time, it must be underscored that Romans 6 itself, according to Roman liturgical sources, was not even used as the epistle reading in the Easter Vigil liturgies until it was placed there in the post–Vatican II liturgical reforms.

Although the Protestant Reformation did little to restore either the prebaptismal catechumenate or Easter baptism itself, the baptismal imagery of Romans 6 appears to have enjoyed a bit of a rebirth in theological importance and emphasis in that era. Certainly the chief proponent of this image was Martin Luther, Augustinian friar and professor of biblical studies. In his 1520 *Babylonian Captivity of the Church,* in which he strongly attacked and challenged the sacramental system of the Western late medieval church, Luther could write:

> Baptism thus signifies two things—death and resurrection, that is, full and complete justification. When the minister immerses the child in the water it signifies death, and when he draws it forth again it signifies life. Thus Paul expounds it in Romans 6 [verse 4]: "We were buried therefore with Christ by baptism into death, so that as Christ was raised from the dead by the glory of the Father, we too might walk in newness of life." This death and resurrection we call the new creation, regeneration and spiritual birth. This should not be understood only allegorically as the death of sin and the life of grace, as many understand it, but as actual death and resurrection. For baptism is not a false sign.[24]

As we shall see in the next section of this chapter, no one in the history of the church, apart from the Fathers of the late fourth century, has had such a profound sense of Paul's Romans 6 theology of baptism and its implications for Christian life *and death* as did Luther, who, in a modern ecumenical context, has been called "our common teacher" by Catholics and Protestants alike. While Protestant Reformers such as Ulrich Zwingli, John Calvin and others, did not ignore this image, none made it the center of their baptismal theology and spirituality in the way that Luther did. It also must be noted, with regard to the sixteenth-century Catholic or Counter Reformation, that no reference to Romans 6 appears in the canons and decrees of the Council of Trent on baptism, and that in the *Catechism of the Council of Trent* (1566) this image is invoked primarily in reference to the lack of punishment due to original sin after biological death itself:

> Baptism also remits all the punishment due to original sin after this life, for through the merit of the death of our Lord, we are able to attain this blessing. By Baptism . . . we die with Christ. *For if,* says the Apostle, *we have been planted together in the likeness of his death, we shall be also in the likeness of his resurrection.*[25]

The Modern Recovery of This Image   As in the church of the late fourth century and in the rather patristic-sounding writings of Luther on baptism, so in our own day Romans 6 has been recovered and restored as the primary image for contemporary celebration, theological reflection, and catechesis on baptism. The very first sentence of the Roman Catholic General Introduction to *Christian Initiation* clearly makes this Pauline image central: "In the sacraments of Christian initiation we are freed from the power of darkness and joined to Christ's death, burial and resurrection."[26] So also, the recent *Catechism of the Catholic Church,* while not ignoring other baptismal images in the least, in a manner quite distinct from that of the *Catechism of the Council of Trent* can say clearly:

> According to the Apostle Paul, the believer enters through Baptism into communion with Christ's death, is buried with him, and rises with him. . . . The baptized have "put on Christ." Through the Holy Spirit, Baptism is a bath that purifies, justifies, and sanctifies.[27]

Perhaps most importantly, the restoration of the adult catechumenate and Easter baptism in the RCIA have themselves made a profound contribution toward the recovery of this image in contemporary post–Vatican II baptismal practice and theology. In the Blessing of Water prayer at the Easter Vigil in the current Roman Rite, for example, even the epiclesis and gift of the Holy Spirit tend to be somewhat subordinated to this image:

> We ask you Father, with your Son
> to send the Holy Spirit upon the waters of this font.
> *May all who are buried with Christ in the death of baptism*
> *rise also with him to newness of life.*[28]

As we shall see in the next chapter, the language of this prayer reflects a deliberate shift in imagery toward Romans 6 from the imagery in the liturgical sources used in its composition.

Ecumenically as well, this image has become again quite dominant. The 1982 ecumenical convergence document, *Baptism, Eucharist, Ministry,* of the Faith and Order Commission of the World Council of Churches makes this image primary in its discussion of the meanings of baptism:

> Baptism means participating in the life, death and resurrection of Jesus Christ. Jesus went down into the river Jordan and was baptized in solidarity with sinners in order to fulfill all righteousness (Matthew 3:15). This baptism led Jesus along the way of the Suffering Servant, made manifest in his sufferings, death and resurrection (Mark 10:38–40, 45). By baptism, Christians are immersed in the liberating death of Christ where their sins are buried, where the "old Adam" is crucified with Christ, and where the power of sin is broken. Thus those baptized are no longer slaves to sin, but free. Fully identified with the death of Christ, they are buried with him and are raised here and now to a new life in the power of the resurrection of Jesus Christ, confident that they will also ultimately be one with him in a resurrection like his (Romans 6:3–11; Colossians 2:13, 3:1; Ephesians 2:5–6).[29]

Similarly, together with Roman Catholic RCIA-influenced and inspired attempts and proposals to restore the adult catechumenate and Easter baptism within the Lutheran,[30] Episcopal[31] and other churches today (e.g., the Presbyterian and United Methodist churches), Romans 6 is encountered surely as the dominant and primary baptismal metaphor in the recently revised liturgical books of those traditions. So, for example, the first sentence in the introductory address to the assembly in the rite of "Holy Baptism" in *Lutheran Book of Worship* can say, in words almost identical to those within the Roman Catholic General Introduction to *Christian Initiation:* "In Holy Baptism our gracious heavenly Father liberates us from sin and death by joining us to the death and resurrection of our Lord Jesus Christ."[32]

Such modern ecumenical recovery of this image, of course, is not simply the legacy of RCIA or other post–Vatican II liturgical developments throughout the churches but was due, primarily, to the developments in biblical, patristic and liturgical scholarship that characterized the liturgical movement itself and so prepared the way for the patristic-based restoration of the contemporary rites of Christian initiation themselves. As early as 1948, French patristics scholar Jean Cardinal Daniélou could write, in words that still serve effectively to describe the theology of Christian liturgy today:

> The Christian faith has only one object, the mystery of Christ dead and risen. But this unique mystery subsists under different modes: it is prefigured in the Old Testament, it is accomplished historically in the earthly life of Christ, it is contained in mystery in the sacraments, it is lived mystically in souls, it is accomplished socially in the church, it is consummated eschatologically in the heavenly kingdom. Thus the Christian has at his disposition several registers, a multi-dimensional symbolism, to express this unique reality. The whole of Christian culture consists in grasping the links that exist between Bible and liturgy, Gospel and eschatology, mysticism and liturgy. The application of this method to scripture is called *exegesis;* applied to liturgy it is called *mystagogy.* This consists in reading in the rites the mystery of Christ, and in contemplating beneath the symbols the invisible reality.[33]

Indeed, it is probably our own age more than any other in the history of the church that can be characterized as the age of the Paschal Mystery in terms of our celebration and interpretation of baptism.

Living "After Death"

Letting death be death and nourished by the voices and liturgical texts in our common traditions, however, we are still left with the question: What are the implications of baptismal death, burial and resurrection in Christ both for the baptized and for the church itself as it struggles to live and witness faithfully in the world? In other words, what does our baptismal plunge into the Mystery of Christ, crucified and risen, mean?

It is not often noted that when St. Paul speaks of baptism in Romans 6, he does not say that we are dead, buried *and risen* already in Christ. Rather, what he *does* say is that we are dead and buried in Christ by baptism with the result that "*if* we have been united with him in a death like his, we *will* certainly be united with him in a resurrection like his" (Romans 6:5, emphasis added). Resurrection thus remains a future reality, one not yet accomplished or fulfilled, but a reality in which we now walk in "newness of life." In other words, for Paul, baptism is really about our participation in the death and burial of Christ in the *hope* of our ultimate resurrection in him. Or, as he writes in Galatians 2:19–20, "I have been crucified with Christ; and it is no longer I who live, but it is Christ who lives in me. And the life I live in the flesh I live by faith in the Son of God, who loved me and gave himself for me," or, as we read in the deutero-Pauline letter to the Colossians (3:3): "For you have died, and your life is hidden with Christ in God."

If the letter to the Colossians moves already toward including our resurrection as part of the baptismal event, Paul's own theology in Galatians and Romans does not.

Clearly for him the profound reality of baptism means that whatever our life is now after baptism or whatever it will be at the resurrection, it is this death and burial, this participation in Christ's crucifixion, death and burial that marks our present, we might say cruciform, existence in the world as the cross of Christ itself continues to characterize and shape that existence.

While this baptismal reality certainly gives rise to those powerful metaphors of conversion to Christ, of constant dying to sin and being raised up to walk in newness of life with and in Christ, of putting to death the "old Adam," and of a life of continual and ongoing conversion, repentance and renewal, one thing is most clear. For St. Paul, the baptized are already dead and buried. Whatever the future holds in Christ, because of baptism, death itself is a reality and experience already *behind* us! And that has profound implications for how the baptized face and embrace the postbaptismal life itself in their cruciform journey toward the resurrection. The powerful word that this baptismal image speaks is this: Because of baptism into Christ *we are already dead!*

Whether part of our modern denial of death, or whether merely indicative of hallucinatory experiences by those on the brink of biological death, a contemporary analogy to baptismal death and subsequent life is certainly suggested by the phenomenon of "near death," "out of the body" or "life after life" experiences apparently so common in today's culture and society. Those who have studied this phenomenon in detail note that those who have "died" and "returned to life" in such a way tend to have both a strong sense of purpose, of what we might call a mission to be completed in life, as well as a strong absence of the fear of death itself. In at least an experiential sense, death is something they have already faced, and they have now been empowered by this experience to begin living what Raymond Moody, Jr. calls "life *after* life."[34]

Isn't something like this precisely what our Romans 6 imagery and theology of baptism have been saying all along? Irene Nowell writes of the rich symbolic meaning of the baptismal waters:

> The primary image for Christians, the image that colors all other reality, is the new exodus, the death and resurrection of Christ, which delivers them from the slavery of death and leads them to the promised land of God's kingdom. That event creates them as a people and gives them life. . . . Baptism is the people's entrance into that saving event, their passage through the waters of death into life. . . . As Christians we stand with death before us *and behind us.* We look back to the death of sin; we look ahead at the waters of baptism beyond which lies the promised land. Only through the waters of chaos, the waters of the flood, the waters of the sea, can we come to life. . . . Only through baptism into Christ's death and resurrection can we hope for a share in the resurrection. Water is a symbol of death; water is a symbol of life. Water has become our way through death to life.[35]

Because of baptism into the death and burial of Christ, the life we now live is quite similarly a "life *after* life" with all kinds of consequences and implications both for how we as Christians might face death itself as well as for how we might embrace our "post-death" baptismal mission and identity as church in the world.

Baptism and the Christian Approach to Death As noted above, apart from the Fathers of the late fourth century, no one has had such a profound sense of Paul's Romans 6 theology of baptism and its implications for Christian life *and death* as did Luther. In his *Small Catechism* (1529), in answer to the question, "What does such baptizing with water signify?" Luther responded:

> It signifies that the old Adam in us, together with all sins and evil lusts, should be drowned by daily sorrow and repentance and be put to death, and that the new man should come forth daily and rise up, cleansed and righteous, to live forever in God's presence.[36]

But, ten years earlier, in his important treatise that merits wide and close reading still today, *The Holy and Blessed Sacrament of Baptism, 1519,* Luther not only allowed death to be death but saw baptism itself as the grand "rehearsal" for death:

> This significance of baptism—the dying or drowning of sin—is not fulfilled completely in this life. Indeed this does not happen until man passes through bodily death and completely decays to dust. As we can plainly see, the sacrament or sign of baptism is quickly over. But the spiritual baptism, the drowning of sin, which it signifies, lasts as long as we live and is completed only in death. Then it is that a person is completely sunk in baptism, and that which baptism signifies comes to pass. . . . Therefore this whole life is nothing else than a spiritual baptism which does not cease until death, and he who is baptized is condemned to die. It is as if the priest, when he baptizes, were to say, "Lo, you are sinful flesh. Therefore I drown you in God's name and in his name condemn you to death, so that with you all your sins may die and be destroyed." Wherefore St. Paul, in Romans 6 [verse 4], says: "We were buried with Christ by baptism into death." The sooner a person dies after baptism, the sooner is his baptism completed. . . . Therefore the life of a Christian, from baptism to the grave, is nothing else than the beginning of a blessed death. For at the Last Day God will make him altogether new. . . . Similarly the lifting up out of the baptismal water is quickly done, but the thing it signifies . . . , even though it begins in baptism, lasts until death, indeed, until the Last Day. Only then will that be finished which the lifting up out of baptism signifies. Then shall we arise from death, from sins, and from all evil, pure in body and soul, and then we shall live eternally. Then shall we be truly lifted up out of baptism and be completely born, and we shall put on the true baptismal garment of immortal life in heaven.[37]

Certainly others, including those in our own day, have approached the question of death in a similar baptismal manner. The late Mark Searle (+1992), professor of liturgical studies at the University of Notre Dame, whose writings on Christian initiation continue to influence all who work in the field, faced his own terminal illness **21** from a strong baptismal faith in the Paschal Mystery. Even his own funeral and burial were exemplary witnesses to the Romans 6 image of baptism itself with, by his own direction, his body dressed for burial in an alb-like baptismal garment, embroidered with a cross, and placed within a simple wooden casket. Searle's own words, very much like those of Luther above, were printed at the beginning of the worship folder for his funeral Mass:

> If . . . we were to learn from the celebration of the paschal mystery to surrender our lives totally to God in Christ, the death of the Christian would be but the further and final rehearsal of a pattern learnt in life and practiced over and over again in a lifetime of liturgical participation. . . . [F]or those who have learnt from the prayers and rituals of the Christian liturgy how to let go of all that we cling to to save ourselves from the void, the final surrender of death will be a familiar and joyous sacrifice.[38]

To offer but one other contemporary and powerful example, one of the great and lasting gifts of the late Joseph Cardinal Bernardin (+1996) to the Archdiocese of Chicago specifically and to all people in general is his best-selling book, *The Gift of Peace*. Here, in his own words, Bernardin demonstrated clearly and movingly his insight "that probably the most important thing [he] could do for the people of the Archdiocese—and everyone of good will—would be the way [he] prepare[d] for death."[39] While explicit references to baptism appear nowhere in Bernardin's personal reflections, the entire book actually unfolds the implications of St. Paul's Romans 6 understanding of baptism for how Christians might face death. He writes:

> As we look upon the cross and recall the specific ways by which people share in its mystery, there are many perspectives to be considered. I will highlight only one: The essential mystery of the cross is that it gives rise to a certain kind of loneliness, an inability to see clearly how things are unfolding, an inability to see that, ultimately, all things will work for our good, and that we are, indeed, not alone. . . . This sense of

being abandoned, this extreme experience of loneliness, is evident in Jesus' cry: "My God, my God, why have you forsaken me?" (Matthew 27:46). If the Lord experienced pain and suffering, can we, as his disciples, expect anything less? No! Like Jesus, we too must expect pain. There is, however, a decisive difference between our pain as disciples and that experienced by those who are *not* the Lord's disciples. The difference stems from the fact that, as disciples, we suffer *in communion with* the Lord. And that makes all the difference in the world! . . . [I]n the final analysis, our participation in the paschal mystery—in the suffering, death and resurrection of Jesus—brings a certain *freedom:* the freedom to let go, to surrender ourselves to the living God, to place ourselves completely in his hands, knowing that ultimately he will win out! The more we cling to ourselves and others, the more we try to control our destiny—the more we lose the sense of our lives, the more we are impacted by the futility of it all. It's precisely in letting go, in entering into complete union with the Lord, in letting him take over, that we discover our true selves. It's in the act of abandonment that we experience redemption, that we find life, peace, and joy in the midst of physical, emotional, and spiritual suffering.[40]

Baptismal Implications for a "Dead" Church in the World

If this baptismal image forms our Christian understanding and response to death itself, then certainly it must also form us in a baptismal way of ongoing life in Christ. If we are truly dead and buried by our baptism into Christ's Paschal Mystery, then we can afford to be a church, a "dead church," which understands itself as already having death in its past and walking in newness of life only as a most gracious, freely given and divine gift. If we as church are truly crucified, dead and buried in Christ so much so that, to paraphrase St. Paul, "it is no longer we who live but Christ who lives in us" (See Galatians 2:20), then there is nothing left to hold on to other than this, nothing left to lose of ourselves and identity that cannot be risked in service to the reign of God as we follow the way of the cross, which we know of and embrace as the only and ultimate way to life. For, if we **23** as church are already dead, then how can even death itself possibly pose a threat to us any longer? Again, it is Cardinal Bernardin's reflections that remind us strongly that the experience of death itself has a way of confronting us with the need to focus only on what is truly essential in life and "how much of what consumes our daily life is trivial and insignificant."[41] Such a baptismal spirituality, such baptismal death mysticism, has profound implications for what we might call a baptismal ecclesiology, a theology of the church itself rooted primarily in our baptismal plunge into the death and burial of Christ.

In his 1977 essay, "Christian Initiation in Post-Conciliar Catholicism: A Brief Report," Aidan Kavanagh wrote:

> I shall take confidence that the restored Roman rites of Christian initiation have begun to come alive when I read a treatise on Christian ethics that begins with baptism into Christ; when I see episcopal meetings deciding on church discipline from a baptismal perspective; when I partake in ecumenical discussions that begin not with Luther or Cranmer or Calvin or Trent, but with baptism; when I am lectured on ministry in terms not of modern sexual roles but of baptism; when I can worship in a parish that consummates its corporate life through Lent at the paschal vigil, gathered around the font where all new life begins.[42]

What kind of church would we be and what kind of Christians would we form if we took our baptismal death as death in Christ seriously, if we, as church, fully aware that we are a "dead church" living after life, chose to focus on what is truly essential in our postbaptismal life? It would be a church much like that already envisioned in *Lumen Gentium* 18, where the church is spoken of as simultaneously holy and in constant need of purification, and where, like all the baptized, the church is called to continual repentance, reform and renewal as it seeks to put the "old Adam" to death daily in order that Christ, and Christ alone, may come to life within it. *Lumen Gentium* 18 states clearly: "The church . . . clasping sinners to her bosom, at once holy and always in need of purification *(sancta simul et semper purificanda),* follows constantly the path of penance and renewal."[43]

It also would be a church for whom the ecumenical end of the scandal of Christian division would be among its highest priorities for the sake of the credibility of its mission and service in the world. In spite of all the conversation, legislation and dialogue in our day and age about the need to preserve our Catholic, Lutheran or other ecclesial identities, the fact of the matter is that baptism already gives us a core, foundational identity. Hence, a church that knows itself as dead and buried in baptism can afford to risk itself ecumenically in the pursuit of full and visible Christian unity because it knows already the common Christian identity it shares, having been brought to newness of life out of a common watery grave. Pope John Paul II, in his important encyclical *Ut Unum Sint,* for example, underscores the baptismal basis for Christian unity precisely in the language of Romans 6, when he asks

> How is it possible to remain divided if we have been "buried" through baptism in the Lord's death, in the very act by which God, through the death of his Son, has broken down the walls of division? Division openly contradicts the will of Christ, provides a stumbling block to the world and inflicts damage on the most holy cause of proclaiming the good news to every creature.[44]

In the same way, I suspect that a church fully aware of its status as dead and buried by baptism into Christ would work passionately to break down the social, economic, ethnic/racial and gender-related walls of division and separation even within itself as it seeks to express ever more concretely the great baptismal vision of equality articulated by St. Paul in Galatians 3:27–28:

> As many of you as were baptized into Christ have clothed yourselves with Christ. There is no longer Jew or Greek, there is no longer slave or free, there is no longer male and female; for all of you are one in Christ Jesus.

Like death itself, which does not respect person, sex, age, status or wealth, baptism also is the "Great Equalizer." Are not racism, classism and sexism but concrete signs of the presence in us of the "old Adam," who must continually be put to death, "drowned" with Christ in the waters of baptism? Hence, a church that knows itself as already dead and buried by baptism into the *one* Christ, who is neither "Jew or Greek . . . slave or free . . . male and female," can dare to "put on" this Christ and risk itself and its identity in the pursuit of a full and inclusive catholicity. Aidan Kavanagh was correct. In such a church that knows itself in baptism as both "at once holy and always in need of purification" (*Lumen Gentium* 18), questions about ethics, ecumenism, ordained and other ministries, liturgical inculturation, language and translations, the identity of the liturgical assembly and its ministers, etc., will always be addressed first from the perspective of having death and burial in Christ already behind us. Only then, in Kavanagh's words, might we "take confidence that the restored . . . rites of Christian initiation have begun to come alive."

Further, such a church, knowing itself as "living after life" would know that its goal is nothing other than to die, than to embrace the cross in its mission of solidarity and service in the world in continuity with Christ's own mission. As noted above, those who have "died" and "returned" from various "near death" experiences in our own day tend to have a renewed and strong sense of purpose, of what we might call a mission to be completed in life. Such a renewed sense of purpose and mission must also mark a "dead" church and certainly a baptismal ecclesiology is an ecclesiology in which such mission is central. From all of the models and images by which one might understand the nature and identity of the church,[45] the best model for a baptismal ecclesiology flowing from Romans 6 is probably that of the church as Servant, a servant people of God involved in Christ's own mission of priestly service in the world. In a pastoral letter to his archdiocese, written in 1966, Richard Cardinal Cushing wrote:

> Jesus came not only to proclaim the coming of the Kingdom, he came also to give himself for its realization. He came to serve, to heal, to reconcile, to bind up wounds. Jesus, we may say, is in an exceptional way the Good Samaritan. He is the one who comes alongside of us in our need and in our sorrow, he extends himself for our sake. He truly dies that we might live and he ministers to us that we might be healed. . . . So it is that the church announces the coming of the Kingdom of God not only in word, through preaching and proclamation, but more particularly in work, in her ministry of reconciliation, of binding up wounds, of suffering service, of healing. . . . As the Lord was the "man for others," so must the church be "the community for others."[46]

Similarly, Lutheran theologian and martyr Dietrich Bonhoeffer wrote in his work *The Cost of Discipleship* that the call of Christ is always a call to death in him:

> When Christ calls a man, he bids him come and die. It may be a death like that of the first disciples who had to leave home and work to follow him. . . . But it is the same death every time—death in Jesus Christ, the death of the old man at his call. Jesus' summons to the rich young man was calling him to die, because only the man who is dead to his own will can follow Christ. In fact every command of Jesus is a call to die, with all our affections and lusts. But we do not want to die, and therefore Jesus Christ and his call are necessarily our death as well as our life. The call to discipleship, the baptism in the name of Jesus Christ means both death and life. . . . If we refuse to take up our cross and submit to suffering and rejection . . . , we forfeit our fellowship with Christ and have ceased to follow him. But if we lose our lives in his service and carry our cross, we shall find our lives again in the fellowship of the cross with Christ. The opposite of discipleship is to be ashamed of Christ and his cross and all the offence which the cross brings in its train. . . . Discipleship means allegiance to the suffering Christ, and it is therefore not at all surprising that Christians should be called upon to suffer. In fact it is a joy and token of his grace.[47]

And, with regard to the mission of the church itself, Bonhoeffer could write in his famous *Letters and Papers from Prison,*

> The church is the church only when it exists for others. To make a start, it should give away all its property to those in need. . . . The church must share in the secular problems of ordinary human life, not dominating but helping and serving.[48]

A church dead and buried by baptism into Christ is liberated from the fear of death itself and, therefore, can dare to risk itself in a mission of suffering service in the world because it knows and seeks to know only the cross and suffering with the world as the way to resurrection. You see, death has a way of setting one free from all kinds of constraints, laws, plans, priorities and old ways of doing things. So, if the church is truly dead and buried in Christ, then there is nothing left to lose in offering itself in service in union and solidarity with the crucified Christ himself. What can possibly happen any longer to an individual or church which knows itself to be dead already? Absolutely nothing! And, as such, the church has been set free by its baptismal death and burial to become truly this community for others in the world.

One in our own day who came to understand the mission of the church and his own episcopal ministry within the church in precisely this way was the Salvadoran martyr Archbishop Oscar Arnulfo Romero (+1980), champion of El Salvador's poor and oppressed. Romero boldly faced the numerous death threats he encountered in response to his ministry in a way that can only be characterized as baptismal: "If they kill me, I shall rise in the Salvadoran people." Only one who knew himself already dead and buried in Christ could make such a bold assertion about his own future. But Romero is not alone. Those who suggest that, rather than the patristic era, it is actually our own time that should be termed the "age of the martyrs" are undoubtedly correct. If Tertullian was right in claiming that the "blood of the martyrs is the seed of the church," then it is also true that this "seed" of the church is precisely that which is planted by our baptismal plunge into Christ's death and burial. From that watery grave emerges a servant community of the cross, which expects nothing other than what its Servant-Master himself endured and experienced. Who knows what kind of church might yet arise when such baptismal-Paschal Mystery imagery is embraced by the baptized themselves? In the words of a contemporary hymn:

> The church of Christ, in every age
> Beset by change, but Spirit led
> Must claim and test its heritage
> And keep on rising from the dead.
>
> Across the world, across the street,
> The victims of injustice cry
> For shelter and for bread to eat
> And never live before they die.
>
> Then let the servant church arise
> A caring church that longs to be
> A partner in Christ's sacrifice
> And clothed in Christ's humanity.
>
> For he alone, whose blood was shed
> Can cure the fever in our blood
> And teach us how to share our bread
> And feed the starving multitude.
>
> We have no mission but to serve
> In full obedience to our Lord;
> To care for all, without reserve,
> And spread his liberating Word.[49]
>   —Fred Pratt Green

Such is the kind of church a baptismal ecclesiology flowing from Romans 6 may well yet engender in our own world.

Conclusion

Baptism as our participation in the death, burial and resurrection of Christ is clearly a powerful, dominant and inviting image for our continual appropriation today. It is, of course, both gift and challenge in what it affirms and in what it calls for in terms of our ongoing life and lifelong conversion by way of response. Our churches have done quite well in restoring this image to prominence in contemporary baptismal celebration, theology, catechesis and, in several notable places, architecture. The Easter Vigil with public baptisms and baptismal renewal at its heart, as part of the whole Paschal Triduum, has been recovered as the very center and heartbeat of the liturgical year. The Lenten season, especially as represented in Year A of the lectionary with its watery Johannine gospel readings and scrutinies and its suggested use for whenever there are catechumens in a given parish, has been restored largely as a period of baptismal preparation for the Vigil itself. And baptisms administered by the preferred mode of immersion in fonts large enough literally to drown in are no longer an exception or seen as elements foreign to our sacramental-liturgical experience and tradition, but part of it. While we could always do a better job liturgically (e.g., Lent is still too often an extended Passion Sunday; baptisms still too often are administered in private with a minimalism of sacramental sign and ritual gesture; and too many fonts still resemble bird baths more than pools or tombs), our current liturgical books provide us textually and ritually with the model of what was envisioned by those who produced these books and what our liturgical experience could be.

Such, of course, is a model well worth pursuing further. For this image of baptism as our participation in the death, burial and resurrection of Christ, as we have seen in this chapter, is an image still with great potential and with numerous implications for forming the baptized themselves as church according to the great Paschal Mystery of Christ himself. Indeed, where would we be without this paschal understanding of baptism?

Having said this, however, it must also be said that Romans 6 is not the only baptismal image at our disposal today. The remaining chapters of this book are devoted to these other images, not in distinction to Romans 6 but in complementarity with it.

CHAPTER 2

Baptism as New Birth and Adoption by Water and the Holy Spirit

■

In those days Jesus came from Nazareth of Galilee and was baptized by John in the Jordan. And just as he was coming up out of the water, he saw the heavens torn apart and the Spirit descending like a dove on him. And a voice came from heaven, "You are my Son, the Beloved; with you I am well pleased." (Mark 1:9–11)

Jesus answered [Nicodemus], "Very truly, I tell you, no one can see the kingdom of God without being born from above." Nicodemus said to him, "How can anyone be born after having grown old? Can one enter a second time into the mother's womb and be born?" Jesus answered, "Very truly, I tell you, no one can enter the kingdom of God without being born of water and Spirit. What is born of flesh is flesh, and what is born of the Spirit is spirit." (John 3:3–6)

But when the goodness and loving kindness of God our Savior appeared, he saved us, not because of any works of righteousness that we had done, but according to his mercy, through the water of rebirth and renewal by the Holy Spirit. This Spirit he poured out on us richly through Jesus Christ our Savior, so that, having been justified by his grace, we might become heirs according to the hope of eternal life. (Titus 3:5)

Contemporary liturgical scholarship on the evolution and theology of baptism has tended to accept a fundamental distinction between baptism as a ritual of regeneration, new birth or adoption "in water and the Holy Spirit" (John 3:5; Titus 3:5), rooted in Jesus' own baptism in the Jordan, as a characteristic emphasis and paradigm of the Eastern liturgical traditions (especially

33

that of early Syria and, quite possibly, early Egypt) and baptism as a ritual of death, burial and resurrection in Christ (Romans 6) as a characteristic emphasis and paradigm of the churches of the West. This acceptance has led several contemporary liturgists to suggest that the theological interpretation of baptism in the West today should attempt to "recover" the early "Eastern" focus on John 3:5 and so come to enrich "Western" baptismal theology as well.

Gerard Austin, for example, writes that "the theology of baptism must be viewed not only under the aspect of dying (Romans 6), but under the aspect of the birth event (John 3) as well. In this regard *the richness of the Eastern tradition* should be tapped."[1]

With regard to infant baptism, in particular, Mark Searle also called for renewed attention to the early Eastern tradition for the recovery of a whole cluster of initiation images having little to do with passing from death to life or with sharing in the dying and rising of Christ through baptism. Such images, noted Searle, include seeing the font as *womb,* rather than tomb; calling the font the "Jordan" itself in some traditions; and interpreting baptism under the metaphors of "adoption, divinization, sanctification, gift of the Spirit, indwelling, glory, power, wisdom, rebirth, restoration [and] mission."[2]

At the end of his recent and detailed study of the baptism of Jesus and its influence in early Christianity, again based primarily in Eastern sources, Kilian McDonnell calls for a "retrieval" of the paradigm of Jesus' baptism and its baptismal theology of new birth in order to "balance" the Romans 6 theological emphasis that the West has inherited.[3] And in my recent book on the evolution and interpretation of the rites of Christian initiation I accepted quite uncritically this supposed East–West distinction and voiced a similar concern about our need to pay closer attention to the Christian East in our Western baptismal theology and practice today.[4]

It is true that baptism as new birth and adoption by "water and the Holy Spirit," modeled on Jesus' own baptism in the Jordan, *is* a characteristic of the early Eastern Christian liturgical traditions. For the Syriac-speaking Christians of East Syria, living in what is modern-day Iraq and Iran, the catechumenate itself was quite minimal both in content and duration, it seems. Baptism itself *may* have taken place on the feast of the Epiphany, understood as the great "Theophany" of Christ in the Jordan, his own baptismal "birth" in the Jordan, a "new birth" rite understood as the means by which the Holy Spirit, especially through a *prebaptismal* anointing, assimilated the neophyte to the messianic priesthood and kingship of Christ.[5]

One document from mid-third century Syria, the *Didascalia Apostolorum,* even suggests that Psalm 2:7, "You are my son: today I have begotten you,"[6] the same verse quoted as a textual variant in the account of Jesus' baptism in Luke 3:22, was recited as part of the baptismal formula. Other third-century documents from this tradition, most notably the Syrian *Apocryphal Acts of the Apostles,* which are of great value as liturgical sources for this period, regularly refer to the Holy Spirit as "Mother,"[7] a theological-baptismal emphasis still to be noted in the baptismal rites of the East Syrian churches (e.g., Assyro-Chaldean and Syro-Malabar) today.[8]

Even for the great Eastern Christian mystagogues of the fourth and fifth centuries, who, as we have seen, tended to move strongly in the direction of Romans 6, this image of rebirth remained an abiding characteristic and came to be synthesized with Romans 6 in their baptismal theologies. In the early Greek- and Coptic-speaking Egyptian Christian tradition—known by Clement and Origen of Alexandria—a forty-day prebaptismal catechumenate commencing on Epiphany, again understood as the feast of Jesus' baptism, seems to have led to baptism on the sixth day of the sixth week of this post-Epiphany fast (sometime in mid-February),[9] and the rite itself appears to have been understood not in terms of death and resurrection imagery but rather as "crossing the Jordan" with our Joshua–Jesus. For Origen, the imagery of baptism had little to do with the Paschal language of crossing the Red Sea or death and burial in Christ. Rather, the Exodus from Egypt signified entrance into the forty-year "catechumenate" of wandering in the wilderness; the Israelites' crossing of the Jordan functioned as the great Old Testament baptismal typology.[10] In fact, as we saw at the beginning of the previous chapter, within the first three centuries of the church's existence it was only among the Latin-speaking Christians of the North African churches and the multi-ethnic groups that made up the Christian communities living in Rome where we begin to encounter both baptism at Easter and the concomitant use of Romans 6 theology to interpret such a practice.

To say that baptism as "new birth" or adoption "by water and the Holy Spirit" is only a characteristically *Eastern* image or focus, however, is simply incorrect; much of contemporary liturgical scholarship on baptism, my own included, needs further nuance in this regard. In spite of the fact that Romans 6 has become the dominant baptismal image in our own day and is often held up as *the* image preferred in the history of the Western liturgical traditions, the image of new birth and adoption is as much Western as it is Eastern. The evidence supplied by the extant *Western* liturgical sources throughout the ages demonstrates that, even within the context of Easter baptism itself, baptism as "new birth" or "adoption" along the lines of John 3:5 is likewise a dominant *Western* baptismal image and paradigm, and that Romans 6 itself is, quite surprisingly, relatively absent from the liturgical sources themselves.

In order to demonstrate this, I provide in the next two major sections of this chapter a collection of several representative texts from extant baptismal liturgies: first, from the patristic through the early medieval periods, as well as *some* theological statements about baptism from other authors, where the liturgical texts themselves are not readily available, and second from various sixteenth-century Protestant Reformers and the Council of Trent. These texts are permitted to stand alone for the reader's own reflection with brief comments provided only at the end of these two sections. The implications of these texts for baptismal practice, theology and spirituality will be addressed in the next section. Finally, in the fourth section I shall make some suggestions related to how this image of baptismal new birth and adoption might be recovered today among us, especially in relationship to the feast of the Baptism of our Lord on the Sunday after the Epiphany.

Latin Patristic and Medieval Liturgical Texts

Rome

1. The *Apostolic Tradition,* ascribed to Hippolytus of Rome (ca. 215)

   Postbaptismal, episcopal hand-laying prayer:

   And the bishop shall lay his hands on them and invoke, saying: Lord God, you have made them worthy to receive remission of sins *through the laver of regeneration of the holy Spirit:* send upon them your grace, that they may serve you according to your will; for to you is glory, to Father and Son with the holy Spirit in the holy church, both now and to the ages of ages. Amen.[11]

2. The Verona (or "Leonine") Sacramentary (sixth century)[12]

   a. The Collect for Pentecost:

   O ineffable and merciful God, grant that the *children of adoption* whom thy Holy Spirit has called unto itself . . . may harbour nothing earthly in their joy, nothing alien in their faith. . . .

b. In the Canon:
We beseech thee graciously to accept this oblation which we offer to thee for these whom thou hast deigned to *regenerate by water and the Holy Spirit,* granting them remission of all their sins. . . .

c. The Blessing of the Font:
. . . Almighty God . . . whose eyes looked down from on high *upon Jordan's stream when John was baptizing* . . . we pray thy holy glory that thy hand may be laid upon this water that thou mayest cleanse and purify the lesser man who shall be baptized therefrom: and that he, putting aside all that is deathly, may be reborn and brought to life again through the new man reborn in Christ Jesus. . . .

3. The Letter of John the Deacon to Senarius (ca. 500):
Chapter 4. And so by the efforts of himself and others the man . . . is next permitted to receive the words of the Creed . . . which was handed down by the Apostles; so that he who a short time before was called simply a catechumen may now be called a competent or elect. For he was *conceived in the womb of Mother church* and now begins to live, even though the time of the *sacred birth* is not yet fulfilled.[13]

4. Roman Baptismal Inscriptions[14]
a. Baptistry of Saint Lawrence in Damaso:
From this noble spring a saving water gushes,
which cleanses all human defilement.
Do you wish to know the benefits of this sacred water?
These streams *give the faith that regenerates.*
Wash away the defilement of your past life in the sacred fountain.

Surpassing joy to share in the life the water brings!
Whoever resorts to this spring abandons earthly
    things
and tramples under foot the works of darkness.

b. Baptistry of the Lateran, ascribed to Sixtus III
    (432–440):
Here a people of godly race are born for heaven;
the Spirit gives them life in the fertile waters.
The Church-Mother, in these waves, bears her children
like virginal fruit she has conceived by the Holy Spirit.

Hope for the kingdom of heaven, *you who are reborn*
    in this spring,
for those who are born but once have no share in the life of
    blessedness.
Here is to be found the source of life, which washes
    the whole universe,
which gushed from the wound of Christ.

Sinner, plunge into the sacred fountain to wash
    away your sin.
The water receives the old man, and in his place
    makes the new man to rise.
You wish to become innocent; cleanse yourself in
    this bath,
whatever your burden may be, Adam's sin or your
    own.

There is no difference between those who are reborn; they
    are one,
in a single baptism, a single Spirit, a single faith.
Let none be afraid of the number of the weight of
    their sins:
those who are born of this stream will be made
    holy.

5. The Gelasian Sacramentary (seventh century)[15]
    a. XXXIV—The Exposition of the Gospels to the
       Elect at the Opening of the Ears: **39**

. . . And so now the Church *being pregnant by your conception,* glories that amidst her festal worship *she labors to bring forth new lives* subject to the Christian law; so that when the day of the venerable Pascha shall come, *being reborn in the laver of baptism,* ye shall be found worthy like all the saints to receive the promised gift of infancy from Christ our Lord. . . .

b. XLIV—Rites of Initiation at the Easter Vigil:

Blessing of the Font: Almighty everlasting God, be present at the mysteries of thy great goodness, be present at thy sacraments, and *for the creation of the new people which the fount of baptism brings forth to thee send down the Spirit of adoption . . .*

Consecration of the Font: . . . open the fount of baptism for the renewal of all nations of the world, that by the command of thy majesty it may receive the grace of thy Only-Begotten by the Holy Spirit: let thy Holy Spirit by the secret admixture of his light *give fecundity to this water prepared for man's regeneration, so that, sanctification being conceived therein, there may come forth from the unspotted womb of the divine font a heavenly offspring, reborn unto a new creature: that grace may be a mother to people of every age and sex, who are brought forth into a common infancy.* . . .

May the font be alive, *the water regenerating,* the wave purifying, so that all who shall be washing in this saving laver by the operation of the Holy Spirit within them may be brought to the mercy of perfect cleansing. . . .

May the power of the Holy Spirit descend into all the water of this font and *make the whole substance of this water fruitful with regenerating power . . .* that every man who enters this *sacrament of regeneration may be reborn in a new infancy* of true innocence.

Postbaptismal (Presbyteral) Anointing: The Almighty God, the Father of our Lord Jesus Christ, who has made thee *to be regenerated of water and the Holy Ghost* . . . , and has given to thee remission of all thy sins, himself anoints thee . . .

Episcopal Handlaying [ad consignandum] Prayer: Almighty God, Father of our Lord Jesus Christ, who hast made thy servants *to be regenerated of water and the Holy Spirit* . . . , and has given them remission of all their sins . . . send upon thy Holy Spirit, the Paraclete . . .

c. XLV—Collects and Prayers at Mass on the [Paschal] Night:

Preface: . . . Mary has rejoiced in her most holy childbirth. The Church rejoices in *the type of the regeneration of her sons.* Thus the blessed fount that flowed from the Lord's side carried away the burdens of our sins so that at these sacred altars the perpetual life *of the new born* might gather living food.

In the Action [canon of the Mass]: . . . Lord, receive this oblation of thy servants and of all thy family, which we offer unto thee *for all whom thou hast deigned to regenerate by water and the Holy Spirit* . . .

North Africa

1. Cyprian of Carthage[16]

   In the gospel according to John: "Unless someone is born of water and the Spirit, he cannot enter the kingdom of God. For that which is born of flesh is flesh, and that which is born of spirit is spirit." Likewise: "Unless you eat the flesh of the Son of Man and drink his blood, you do not have life in you."

2. Quodvultdeus of Carthage

   I am to explain to you the sacraments of the past night and of the present holy Creed. . . . For you are not yet *reborn in holy baptism,* but by the sign of the cross you have been *conceived in the womb of holy mother church.* . . . [17]

3. Augustine of Hippo

In infants, who are baptized, the *sacrament of regeneration* is given first, and if they maintain a Christian piety, conversion also in the heart will follow, of which the mysterious sign had gone before in the outward body.[18]

Now the *regenerating Spirit* is possessed in common both by the parents who present the child, and by the infant that is presented and is *born again.* . . . [19]

North Italy

1. Ambrose of Milan[20]

De Sacramentis. 2.24: Therefore, thou didst dip, thou camest to the priest. What did he say to thee? "God the Father Almighty . . . who hath *regenerated thee by water and the Holy Ghost,* and hath forgiven thee thy sins, himself anoint thee unto eternal life. . . .

De Sacramentis 3.5: There are, however, some who say and try to urge that this [footwashing] ought to be done, not as a sacrament, not at baptism, not at the regeneration; but only as we should wash the feet of a guest.

De Mysteriis 5: After this, the Holy of holies was unbarred to thee, thou didst enter the *shrine of regeneration* . . .

2. The Ambrosian Manual[21]

Prayers at the Blessing of the Font: Almighty, everlasting God, be present at the mysteries of thy great goodness, be present at thy sacraments, and for the creation *of the new people which the fount of baptism brings forth to thee,* send down the Spirit of adoption . . .

Another Prayer: Look . . . with favor upon sinners, and loose the captive. Restore the innocence which

Adam lost in Paradise. . . . May they receive the likeness of God, which once was lost by envy of the serpent; may the iniquities which follow upon their disobedience be carried away in this pure stream. May they rise up unto rest: may they be brought forward unto pardon, that being renewed in the mystic waters they may know themselves to be redeemed *and reborn* . . .

Postbaptismal Chrismation: Almighty God, the Father of our Lord Jesus Christ, who has *regenerated you by water and the Holy Ghost,* and who has given you remission of all your sins, himself anoints you . . .

Exorcism of the Oil: I exorcize thee, creature of oil . . . that to all who are anointed therewith it *may be unto the adoption of the sons of God* . . .

Prayer: . . . Lead him to the *laver of the second birth,* that with thy faithful people he may be worthy to receive the eternal rewards of thy promises.

Exorcism of Water: . . . when he has been *born again of water and the Holy Ghost* . . . let him become a temple of the living God . . .

Prayer after Baptism: Almighty, everlasting God, who hast *regenerated thy servant N. by water and the Holy Ghost* . . . , and who has given him remission of all his sins, grant him an abiding wisdom . . .

3. Zeno of Verona (+ circa 372)
    Sermons, Bk. II. 29. 1–3: Paschal Sermon: (1) Welcome, my brothers in Christ, *born today!* . . . [Y]our old self has been happily condemned so that he may be forgiven, buried in the wave of the sacred waters so that he may be *quickened in the nest of the womb* and taste the privileges of the resurrection . . . . (2) Oh what goodness of our God! What pure love of our good *mother.* She has taken people different in race, **43**

sex, age, and rank. . . . (3) And lest she should seem to love anyone more or less than another, she grants to all *one birth,* one milk, one pay, one honor of the Holy Spirit. . . . Indeed blessed is the one who always remembers that he is *reborn;* more blessed is the one who does not remember what he was before he was *reborn;* most blessed is the one who does not spoil his infancy with the advance of years.[22]

Sermons, Bk. I.55: To the Neophytes: Why do you stand there, different in race, age, sex, and rank, who soon will be one? Hasten to the *fountain of the sweet womb of your ever-virgin mother* and there know in your nobility and faith that, as one believes, so one will possess blessedness. Oh what a marvelous and truly divine, most blessed honor, in which *she who gives birth does not groan, and the one born never cries!* This is renewal, this is resurrection, this is eternal life, *this is the mother of all,* who has united us, brought us together from every race and nation and straight-way made us one body.[23]

Sermons, Bk. II.28: Invitation to the Font: Come on, why do you stand there, brothers? Through your faith *the life-giving water has conceived you, through the mysteries now it gives birth to you.* Hurry as quickly as you can to what you desire. Behold, now the solemn hymn is sung, *behold soon the sweet crying of infants is heard; behold from the single womb of their parent proceeds a dazzling throng. It is a new thing, that each one is born in a spiritual manner. Run freely to your mother who has no labor if she gives birth to more than she can number. Come in, then, come in, all of you happy ones, in a moment to be babes at the breast together.*[24]

Sermons, Bk. I.32: Invitation to the Font: Rejoice, brothers in Christ, hasten with all desire and receive the heavenly gifts. *Now the saving warmth of the ever-lasting font invites you,* now our mother adopts you so that she may give birth to you, but not in the manner in which your mothers bore you when they brought you into the world, themselves groaning with birth pains and you, waling, filthy, done up in filthy swaddling clothes and surrendered to this world, but with joy and gladness . . . and she freed you from all your sins, and she feeds you not in a stinking cradle but with delight from the sweet-smelling rails of the holy altar, through our Lord Jesus Christ.[25]

Gaul (Eighth Century)

1. *The Missale Gothicum*[26]

    a. Collects for the Blessing of the Fonts:

. . . the Holy Spirit has brought them on a fair course. Let us therefore pray our Lord God to bless this font, that to all who go down therein it may be a *laver of rebirth* unto the remission of all their sins . . .

O God, who for the salvation of souls didst sanctify the waters of Jordan, may there descend upon these waters the angel of thy blessing, that thy servants over whom it has been poured may receive remission of their sins, and being *born again of water and the Holy Spirit* . . . may serve thee faithfully for ever.

    b. A Collect (after Baptism):

. . . let us pray to our Lord and God for his neophytes who are now baptized, that when the Saviour shall come in his majesty he may clothe with the garments of eternal salvation those whom *he has regenerated with water and the Holy Spirit.*

    c. Another Collect (after Baptism):

For those who are baptized, who seek the chrism, who are crowned in Christ, to whom *our Lord has been pleased to grant a new birth,* let us beseech Almighty God that they may bear the baptism they have received spotless unto the end.

d. Immolatio (Eucharistic Preface):
. . . For this is the night which has knowledge of the saving sacraments, the night in which thou dost offer pardon to sinners, *dost make new men from old, from worn out old men dost restore full-grown infants, whom thou dost bring from the sacred font renewed unto a new creature. On this night thy people are new born* and brought forth unto eternal day, the halls of the kingdom of heaven are thrown open, by thy blessed ordinance human conversation is changed to divine.

2. The Bobbio Missal[27]

a. Order for Making a Christian (A Collect)
. . . hear him who bows his head before thee, let him approach *the baptism of the fount of regeneration by water and the Holy Spirit,* who with the Father and the Son liveth and reigneth.

b. Blessing of Waters:
It is meet and right, Almighty God, who hast opened unto us a fount of eternal life and *hast regenerated us by thy Holy Spirit,* to whom thou hast committed this holy laver unto the remission of sins, that it might *be a laver of water in the Holy Spirit* through whom thou dost take from us every stain. . . . [W]e pray thee, O God our Almighty Father, that thou wouldest send down the Holy Spirit upon this water, that whomsoever we shall baptize . . . thou wilt purify and regenerate, and receive into the number of thy saints, and in thy Holy Spirit take them up into life everlasting.

c. Postbaptismal Anointing Prayer:
May God the Father of our Lord Jesus Christ, *who hath regenerated thee by water and the Holy Spirit,* and who hath given thee remission of sins through the laver of regeneration and of blood, himself anoint thee with his holy chrism unto eternal life.

d. After Baptism:
Lord God Almighty, who hast commanded that these thy servants shall *be reborn of water and the Holy Spirit,* preserve in them the holy baptism which they have received and perfect them in the hallowing of thy Name . . .

What is most illuminating in the texts quoted above is the liturgical evidence from Rome in the patristic and early medieval documents. Contrary to what might be expected on the basis of current assumptions, there is almost no reference whatsoever to a Romans 6 theology in these texts! Romans 6 simply does not appear anywhere in the *Apostolic Tradition,* the *Letter of John the Deacon to Senarius,* the *Verona Sacramentary* or the Roman baptismal inscriptions. Furthermore, I can find only one allusion to Romans 6 throughout all of the initiation materials included within the *Gelasian Sacramentary,* where, in the context of the *redditio symboli* (the "return of the Creed"), after referring to the completion of Christ's resurrection in the baptized, it states that "in it [baptism] is celebrated as a kind of death and resurrection."[28] But it is certainly not the dominant interpretative metaphor for baptism throughout this document. Rather, John 3, together with some allusion to Jesus' baptism in the Jordan in the prayers for the blessing of the font, is the central image.

Similarly, while the North African tradition had certainly known the theology of Romans 6 in relationship to baptism since the time of Tertullian's *De baptismo,* John 3 remains an important and complementary image even within this tradition. So also is this the case with Ambrose of Milan and the later Ambrosian-Milanese tradition. If anyone had a Romans 6 understanding of the baptismal submersion or immersion, it was Ambrose of Milan, who, like Cyril (or John) of Jerusalem, related the threefold baptismal dipping to Jesus' three days in the tomb and referred as well to the "tomb-like" shape of the Milanese baptistry. Yet, liturgically, it is Ambrose himself who gives us our first clear reference to the Western postbaptismal anointing prayer which, from that time on at least, will explicitly quote John 3:5 as an integral part of the anointing formula in most Western traditions. Elsewhere in North Italy, at least in the sermons of Zeno of Verona, the imagery of John 3:5 appears to be even more prominent. When all of these texts are combined with the extant eighth-century texts of the Gallican liturgical tradition, where this image is even more pronounced,[29] one is led to ask just how dominant in and characteristic of the Western liturgical traditions, in fact, *is* this so-called "Western theological focus" on Romans 6 as the dominant metaphor for baptism, and when was it that it became such? In liturgical *texts,* at least, it is John 3:5, not Romans 6, which appears to be the preferred baptismal image in the West.

As I suggested in the previous chapter, the practice of Christian initiation in the context of the Easter Vigil may have brought to the rites an added theological focus from a Romans 6 perspective, and so functioned as baptism's overall hermeneutical or interpretative context, and various theologians like Ambrose of Milan may have preferred to use a Romans 6 interpretation of baptism. But such an interpretation does not seem to have had much, if any, direct effect on Western liturgical-baptismal *texts* themselves. Surely that is most significant.

Select Reformation-Era Baptismal Texts

Martin Luther

Flood Prayer (1523): Almighty eternal God, who according to thy righteous judgment didst condemn the unbelieving world through the flood and in thy great mercy didst preserve believing Noah and his family, and who didst drown hardhearted Pharoah with all his host in the Red Sea and didst lead thy people Israel through the same on dry ground, thereby prefiguring this bath of thy baptism, and *who through the baptism of thy dear Child, our Lord Jesus Christ, hast consecrated and set apart the Jordan and all water* as a salutary flood and a rich and full washing away of sins: We pray through the same thy boundless mercy that thou wilt graciously behold this N. and bless him with true faith in the spirit so that by means of this saving flood all that has been born in him from Adam and which he himself has added thereto may be drowned in him and engulfed, and that he may be sundered from the number of the unbelieving, preserved dry and secure in the holy ark of Christendom, serve thy name at all times fervent in spirit and joyful in hope, so that with all believers he may be made worthy to attain eternal life according to thy promise; through Jesus Christ our Lord. Amen.[30]

Postbaptismal Garment Prayer (1526): The almighty God and Father of our Lord Jesus Christ, *who hath regenerated thee through water and the Holy Ghost* and hath forgiven thee all thy sin, strengthen thee with his grace to life everlasting. Amen. Peace be with thee.[31]

A Rite of Baptism, Used at Strassburg, 1525–30

Prayer before Our Father and Apostles' Creed: . . . Let us pray . . . that the Lord will baptize him with water and the Holy Spirit, so that the outward washing which he will perform through me will inwardly be fulfilled in deed and in truth by the Holy Spirit; for that *second birth* which is signified **49** by baptism takes place in *water and in the Holy Spirit,* as the Lord says in John 3.

Prayer after the Apostles' Creed: . . . seal and confirm his heart in the same with the Holy Spirit according to thy Son's promise, so that thy inward renewal and *regeneration of the Spirit* may truly be signified by this our baptism. . . .[32]

Thomas Cranmer and the *Books of Common Prayer* (1549, 1552)

Introduction: Dear[ly] beloved, forasmuch as all men be *conceived and born in sin,* and that no man born in sin can enter into the kingdom of God *(except he be regenerate and born anew of water and the Holy Ghost)* I beseech you to call upon God the Father through our Lord Jesus Christ, that of his bounteous mercy he will grant to these children that thing, which by nature they cannot have, that is to say, they may be baptized with the Holy Ghost, and received into Christ's holy church, and be made lively members of the same.[33]

Postbaptismal Anointing (1549): Almighty God, the Father of our Lord Jesus Christ, *who hath regenerated thee by water and the Holy Ghost,* and hath given unto thee remission of all thy sins, he vouchsafe to anoint thee with the unction of his Holy Spirit, and bring thee to the inheritance of everlasting life. Amen.[34]

The Council of Trent

The Catechism of the Council of Trent (1566): With regard to the definition of Baptism although many can be given from sacred writers, nevertheless that which may be gathered from the words of our Lord recorded in John, and of the Apostle to the Ephesians, appears most appropriate and suitable.

Unless, says our Lord, *a man be born again of water and the Holy Ghost, he cannot enter into the kingdom of God;* and speaking of the Church, the Apostle says, *cleansing it by the laver of water in the word of life.* Thus it follows that Baptism may be rightly and accurately defined: *The Sacrament of regeneration by water in the word.* By nature we are born from Adam children of wrath, but by Baptism we are regenerated in Christ, children of mercy. For He gave power to men *to be made the sons of God, to them that believe in his name, who are born, not of blood, nor of the will of the flesh, nor of the will of man, but of God.*[35]

The above selection of texts from the sixteenth-century Protestant and Catholic Reformations points in a similar direction toward John 3 as a dominant baptismal image as well. While, as we saw in the previous chapter, Romans 6 was clearly Martin Luther's own preferred interpretative text for baptismal theology, apart from possible allusion to it in his *Flood Prayer,* Romans 6 is not clearly present in either his 1523 or 1526 baptismal reforms. Similarly, versions of the traditional presbyteral postbaptismal anointing prayer with their quotation of John 3:5, whether with or without anointing, tended to continue in some way throughout the reformed rites of the sixteenth century and even into modern baptismal rites until the most recent reforms. Is it not, in fact, part of the Protestant Reformation rejection of the "sacrament" of confirmation to argue that baptism itself, as "new birth in water and the Holy Spirit," constituted the "fullness" of Christian initiation in the first place? Hence, nothing else was needed to "complete" baptism. And even the *Catechism of the Council of Trent,* it must be noted, makes *this* image of regeneration and new birth the exclusive baptismal image in its very definition of baptism. So much for Romans 6 as the preferred *Western* baptismal image in the liturgical tradition!

Implications

Several implications arise from this collection of Western baptismal texts and theological comments, namely: (a) the baptismal theology of John 3:5 is as much "Western" as it is "Eastern;" (b) the celebration of baptism at Easter is not incompatible with a baptismal theology based on John 3:5; (c) The principle of *lex orandi, lex credendi* suggests a theology of baptism as "new birth" in the West; and (d) a different approach to baptismal spirituality flowing from John 3 rather than Romans 6 is suggested. Each of these calls for additional comment.

The Baptismal Theology of John 3:5 is as much "Western" as it is "Eastern"   The clear and persistent presence of a John 3:5 theology of baptism, as well as reference to Jesus' baptism in the Jordan, in Western baptismal texts suggests that neither liturgical scholarship nor liturgical renewal need always look to the East to "balance out" the so-called characteristic "Western" theological emphasis on Romans 6. Such "balance," including the several and diverse images that Searle called for in his discussion of infant baptism, are a clear and definite component of the Western liturgical tradition of baptism as well.

As the modern rites of Christian initiation demonstrate, however, an "Easternization" or "Byzantinization" of Western initiation has certainly taken place throughout the various churches today.[36] Perhaps nowhere is this clearer than in the 1971 Roman revision of confirmation, where the Syro-Byzantine formula, "N., be sealed with the gift of the Holy Spirit" has been adopted, an adoption also paralleled in the current baptismal rites of almost every other Western liturgical tradition today. This has tended to overshadow the traditional—and already *pneumatic*—Western "handlaying" prayer for the sevenfold Spirit gift. At the same time, with the exception of the baptismal rite in the Lutheran Church–Missouri

Synod's 1982 publication of *Lutheran Worship*,[37] there has been a systematic excision from Western baptismal rites of the traditional postbaptismal "anointing" prayer, *the* prayer, which, since the time of Ambrose of Milan, has underscored the unitive and integral John 3:5 theology of being begotten in baptism "through water *and* the Holy Spirit." In fact, it is *precisely* a version of this classic prayer and anointing in the Roman Rite which, in the initiation of adults, is regularly omitted in favor of the confirmation chrismation itself! While looking to the East is ecumenically laudable and the attempt to complement or balance a Romans 6 theology with the "richness" of other metaphors, paradigms, and images is surely desirable, the West need not *always* look to the East for the recovery of such a pneumatological baptismal focus. Rather, the West needs to look at and recover the richness of its own tradition as that richness is expressed already within its own classic liturgical texts. The often-decried Western "lack of pneumatology," then, is perhaps due, in part, to the failure of the West to pay adequate attention to its own rich textual liturgical and theological tradition, where, with regard to the rites of Christian initiation at least, such an emphasis is anything but lacking.

The Celebration of Baptism at Easter Is Not Incompatible with a Baptismal Theology Based on John 3:5   The real or ideal, or real but short-lived[38] practice of Easter baptism in the West, while hermeneutically significant in context, does not mean, *necessarily,* the replacement of, or preference for, the baptismal metaphor of Romans 6 for, or over, John 3:5 in the Western liturgical tradition. In his study of baptism and Easter in Zeno of Verona, for example, Gordon Jeanes notes the uneasy juxtaposition of John 3:5 and Romans 6 in Zeno's baptismal sermons:

> Death to the old self and to the world and condemnation of sin are presented in the liturgical formulae of renunciations. **53**

Their meaning and emphasis are amplified by the sermons. But Zeno does not integrate Romans 6 with this imagery, nor does he manage to integrate fully the two ideas of the font as the life-giving womb of Mother Church and as the place of dying and rising. For him the font is still essentially the life-giver and the death dealing is normally restricted to the preparatory rites. . . . In the Church of the second and third centuries baptism was about being born of water and the Spirit, about cleansing and enlightenment. Dying with Christ was not to the fore, even in the West where the custom of baptism at Easter might easily have suggested it. That motif was taken up by the martyr literature, and only when martyrs belonged to the past was it freed for the liturgy and became part of the Church's new definition of itself over against the world. . . . Zeno lived just at the time when this change of understanding was happening, and we see in his sermons the two theologies sitting, slightly uncomfortably, side by side.[39]

At the same time, however, all of the references to baptism in the later *Gelasian Sacramentary* itself appear within the overall context of the *Lenten* catechumenate and *Easter* baptism. But still at that date, as we have seen, the dominant image for what is to take place, or what is taking place at baptism itself, remains John 3:5 and not Romans 6. Such would seem to suggest that the actual occasion for the celebration of Christian initiation, i.e., Easter, either had very little overall influence on the developing shape and theology of Christian initiation in the West or that the theology of John 3:5, as well as Jordan imagery, was too well ingrained in the Western tradition to be displaced by this emphasis. That is, it is not simply that John 3:5 complements or balances Romans 6 in the Western sources but, at least in the extant Roman liturgical texts, it is the relative absence of a Romans 6 theology altogether—even at *Easter*— that must be noted!

With regard to this, one must wonder exactly what has led contemporary liturgical scholars and reformers to opt for a Romans 6 theology of baptism as a "normative" and characteristically "Western" theological focus so much so that contemporary Western liturgical revision of Christian initiation has given Romans 6 a normative status for celebrating and interpreting those rites.

So strong is this modern assumption, in fact, that there is even evidence to suggest that in contemporary liturgical reform there has been a deliberate attempt to downplay or delete entirely the new-birth imagery of John 3:5 in favor of the paschal imagery of Romans 6. For example, after a detailed analysis of the prayer for the blessing of the baptismal water in the *Gelasian Sacramentary* and its use as a source for the blessing of the baptismal water at the Easter Vigil in the current Roman rite, Dominic Serra notes that it is *precisely* the *Gelasian* references to John 3:5 that have been omitted! The particular section of the blessing prayer in question concerns the language in that prayer surrounding the immersion of the Paschal candle into the font:

> We ask you Father, with your Son
> to send the Holy Spirit upon the waters of this font.
> May all who are buried with Christ in the death of baptism
> rise also with him to newness of life.[40]

But the corresponding language for this in the *Gelasian Sacramentary,* as already seen in the selected texts printed above, says quite explicitly that this rite is about fertility and regeneration:

> May the power of the Holy Spirit descend into all the water of this font and make the whole substance of this water fruitful with regenerating power . . . that every man who enters this sacrament of regeneration may be reborn in a new infancy of true innocence.

In specific reference to this, Serra writes:

> [T]he new blessing utilizes only those sections of the Roman epiclesis that do not mention the metaphor of rebirth, and . . . the phrases borrowed from *Ge[lasianum]* 448 have been rewritten so that rebirth images are transformed into paschal references. . . . This sort of substitution is very apparent in the phrases that surround the optional immersion of the paschal candle. . . . The Gelasian text includes a request that

the Spirit render the water fecund for regenerating, while the new blessing asks that "all who are buried with Christ in the death of baptism rise also with him to newness of life." . . . Once again, we have an obvious substitution of a paschal referent for a regeneration image. . . . These substitutions and omissions have the effect of transforming the Gelasian prayer, which was based almost entirely on the metaphor of rebirth, into a prayer based almost exclusively on the paschal dimension of baptism. . . . A clue to understanding this suppression of the rebirth metaphor and its replacement with paschal symbolism can be found in the explanatory note about the candle immersion in the *relatio* on the blessing of the baptismal water in *Schema* 112. The note indicates that the reformers were intent upon emphasizing the paschal and Christic symbolism of the candle, thus avoiding any possible phallic interpretation in the rite of candle immersion. In fact, they decided to change the meaning of the texts surrounding this ritual gesture in order to give the candle immersion the meaning of burial and resurrection with Christ.[41]

Nevertheless, in spite of this, baptism as this sacrament of new birth through water and the Holy Spirit does remain somewhat within, at least, the current Roman baptismal rite. The prayer for the blessing of the waters evokes this image as well as that of death and resurrection:

> In the waters of the Jordan your Son was baptized by John and anointed with the Spirit. . . . By the power of the Holy Spirit give to this water the grace of your Son, so that in the sacrament of baptism all those whom you have created in your likeness may be cleansed from sin and rise to a new birth of innocence by water and the Holy Spirit.[42]

In a similar manner, the first part of the formula that accompanies the postbaptismal anointing also points to this understanding of baptism: "The God of power and Father of our Lord Jesus Christ has freed you from sin and *brought you to new life through water and the Holy Spirit*."[43] And not to be overlooked is the postbaptismal clothing with the white garment—"(N. and N.) you have become a new creation, and have clothed yourselves in Christ"[44]—which may evoke precisely that "new nature" and "image" of Christ himself now given by the Spirit in the baptismal rite of adoption. But this is not a dominant image in the current rite by any means.

Accepting the normativity of Romans 6 as *the* baptismal paradigm for the West and for contemporary Western liturgical reform, then, appears to be a conclusion based on other than explicit and traditional Western *liturgical* grounds. Such grounds include, I would suggest:

(1) the recovery of John 3:5 and Jesus' baptism in the Jordan as the dominant metaphors for baptism in the early Syrian East and the assumption of a different overall focus in the West;

(2) the overwhelming focus on Romans 6 in the interpretative catecheses of Cyril of Jerusalem, John Chrysostom, and Theodore of Mopsuestia (and the resultant shift in baptismal theology in the East) and the *De Sacramentis* and *De Mysteriis* of Ambrose of Milan for the West;

(3) the modern "recovery" of this "Paschal Mystery," as expressed precisely in the writings of these fourth-century mystagogues, as the primary and normative paradigm for Christian life in general;

(4) the concomitant modern restoration of the Easter Vigil as the prime time for baptism in the West, in accord with the early Western liturgical— if not theological—tradition;

(5) the resultant re-reading of Western liturgical sources based on this "recovery" and "restoration"; and

(6) even a fear of allowing the reproductive and sexual images of baptism from the liturgical tradition to speak in a modern context.

But in no case, let me underscore, does this "Western" focus or "recovery" appear to be based on the dominant imagery within the liturgical texts of the traditional baptismal rites themselves! And with this, it seems that "Paschal Mystery" language and metaphor say much more about our *modern* theological approaches to baptism and sacramental theology in general, and *modern* attempts to read the early Western liturgical tradition through paschal eyes than it does about the classic tradition at all, especially as that tradition is expressed within its liturgical texts.

The Principle of *Lex orandi, Lex credendi* in the West suggests a Theology of Baptism as New Birth Whatever Prosper of Aquitaine's famous formula *ut legem credendi statuat lex supplicandi* ("that the law of supplicating may constitute the law of believing")—a phrase often abbreviated as *lex orandi, lex credendi* in popular usage—may or may not mean in relationship to liturgy as a theological and doctrinal source, if a church's theology of baptism *(lex credendi)* is to be read on the basis of the liturgical texts used in its celebration *(lex orandi),* then it seems quite clear that at the very least traditional *Western* theologies of baptism are clearly as expressive of baptism as "adoption, divinization, sanctification, gift of the Spirit, indwelling, glory, power, wisdom, rebirth, restoration, [and] mission" as are those of the Christian East. While a given Church's *lex orandi* cannot and should not be read solely on the basis of liturgical texts, it should be noted that within the ancient East Syrian tradition itself, Paschal baptism also became the (theoretical) norm but never in the sense that its primary theological interpretation of baptism departed too far from either John 3:5 or Jesus' baptism as the dominant paradigms, with the prebaptismal anointing itself, even today, retaining much of its classic pneumatological and "Holy Spirit as Mother" emphasis.[45] Similarly, if the architectural shape of baptismal fonts has anything to say theologically, then it also may be contextually signficant that even in the West evidence of circular "womb-like" fonts and fonts clearly designed to resemble female genitalia (at least in North Africa,[46] the very place of the first reference to *Paschal* baptism) have been uncovered.

If baptism is about death, burial and tombs, it also is about fertility, conception, wombs and births. As such, even sexual-reproductive metaphors, and/or potentially phallic imagery with regard to the Paschal candle itself, are part of our baptismal-liturgical heritage and tradition. Indeed, sacramental liturgy is about all of the deepest currents in life, and certainly those deep currents in human life include sexuality and even sexual imagery! Obviously both the Fathers and the guardians of the classic liturgical traditions of the West understood that and were content to allow such images to remain.

A Different Approach to Baptismal Spirituality   As underscored in the previous chapter, a Christian spirituality based on baptism as death, burial and resurrection in Christ is one powerful way of articulating a way of Christian identity, life and service. A spirituality based on the new birth theology of John 3 or on images of baptismal adoption is yet another. For one spirituality, Christ's own death and resurrection is of paramount importance. For the other spirituality, the Incarnation itself is viewed as salvific, as, for example, in the famous words of Athanasius in the *Incarnation of the Word,* "God became what we are so that we could be made what he is."[47] That is, through *baptism* we become by adoption what Christ is by nature. For one spirituality, baptism is the *tomb* in which the sinful self is put to death in Christ. For the other spirituality, baptism is the *womb* through which the Mothering Spirit of God gives new birth and new life. For one spirituality, sinful Adam is to be put to death. For the other spirituality, Adam is a prisoner and is to be sought after and rescued from sin, death and bondage. For one spirituality, Easter is *the* feast par excellence, the very center of the liturgical year. For the other spirituality, it is the Theophany of Christ in the Jordan at Epiphany, the very manifestation of the Trinity in the waters of the font, that assumes great importance. How one thinks of baptism will shape how one views Christian life and identity. Even if these two views are not mutually contradictory or exclusive, they did and do shape distinct emphases and orientations in the history of the church to which we should pay attention still today.

What would it mean for our life in Christ to recover this image of new birth and adoption, to recover this sense of our baptismal identity as having become by gracious adoption what Christ himself is by divine nature? What might it mean to say in our catechesis of parents who present their children for baptism, that in a real sense they are presenting "their" children for "adoption" into a whole new family network of relationships in which their own parental claims become relativized? What might such mean for the identity, nature and mission of the church in the world, empowered by the baptismal Spirit, which understands itself to be so closely united with Christ that, as the very body of Christ, it shares in the divine nature? It was Pope St. Leo I, who, in one of his Christmas homilies, spoke of the importance of realizing this baptismal–incarnational identity of our sharing in the very nature of Christ:

> Christian, remember your dignity, and now that you share in God's own nature, do not return by sin to your former base condition. Bear in mind who is your head and of whose body you are a member. Do not forget that you have been rescued from the power of darkness and brought into the light of God's kingdom. Through the sacrament of baptism you have become a temple of the Holy Spirit. Do not drive away so great a guest by evil conduct and become again a slave to the devil, for your liberty was bought by the blood of Christ.[48]

What, further, might it mean for the church with regard to its role and identity as "Mother Church," who in the womb of the font is actively involved in the baptismal process of reproduction and birth? As the words from the great Lateran baptistry still proclaim to all who read them today:

> Here a people of godly race are born for heaven;
> the Spirit gives them life in the fertile waters.
> The Church-Mother, in these waves, bears her children
> like virginal fruit she has conceived by the Holy Spirit.

And what might close attention to this image mean for how we come to image God in our own day, especially with regard to the Holy Spirit, who functions *maternally* as "the Lord, the Giver of life" especially in baptism?

Much is to be gained in terms of our sense of Christian identity and spirituality from renewed attention to this image in our baptismal celebration, catechesis and mystagogy today. But, if we have done quite well in restoring a paschal-oriented, Romans 6 baptismal consciousness, we have allowed the image of new birth and adoption to play at best a secondary role, in spite of the fact, as we have seen, that within our classic liturgical traditions this image has been anything but secondary. How little this image of new birth and adoption has been part of our modern baptismal consciousness is surely illustrated within the World Council of Churches' statement on *Baptism, Eucharist, Ministry,* where this image merits only a passing reference and does not even serve as one of the five dominant images that are treated in detail. The *Catechism of the Catholic Church* is not much better in this regard, although it does refer to rebirth and adoption more than *Baptism, Eucharist, Ministry.* Such is an unfortunate development, and the following section of this chapter is concerned with how this image might be recovered more fully for the church today.

Toward the Recovery of This Image Today

If baptism as new birth or adoption through water and the Holy Spirit is easily compatible with baptism as death, burial and resurrection in Christ, with new birth language **61** functioning often as a parallel equivalent to resurrection or newness of life in this context (i.e., baptism as a passage from death to rebirth in Christ), certainly baptismal new birth and/or adoption imagery can also stand on its own without recourse to paschal imagery. Certainly one of the ways to underscore this image today is to consider seriously the Sunday after the Epiphany (January 6), the festival of the Baptism of our Lord, as a most suitable occasion for the celebration and renewal of baptism within the context of the liturgical year. *The Book of Occasional Services* of the Episcopal Church, USA, in fact, provides as a model a complete baptismal vigil for this feast.[49]

Following the service of light or *lucernarium* from Evening Prayer and the opening prayer of the feast itself, this Vigil for the Eve of the Baptism of Our Lord continues with at least three of the following suggested readings, together with their appointed psalms or canticles:

> Genesis (7:1−5, 11−18); 8:6−18; 9:8−13 (The Story of the Flood)
>
> Isaiah 43:15−19 (The Lord Who Makes a Way in the Sea)
>
> Leviticus 8:1−12 (The Washing of Aaron)
>
> 1 Samuel 16:1−13 (The Anointing of David)
>
> 2 Kings 5:1−14 (The Cleansing of Naaman in the Jordan)
>
> Isaiah 55:1−11 (Salvation Offered Freely to All)
>
> Ezekiel 36:24−28 (A New Heart and a New Spirit)
>
> Isaiah 61:1−9 (The Spirit of the Lord Is upon Me)
>
> Isaiah 42:1−9 (Behold My Servant)
>
> 1 Peter 3:15b−22 (When God's Patience Waited in the Days of Noah)
>
> Acts 10:34−38 (God Anointed Jesus with the Holy Spirit)

Following the reading of the gospel (either Matthew 3:13−17; Mark 1:7−11; Luke 3:15−16, 21−22; or Matthew

28:1–10, 16–20) and the sermon or homily, baptism, confirmation and/or a renewal of baptismal vows takes place before the liturgy itself, of course, culminates in the celebration of the eucharist.

The celebration of baptism on Epiphany, with the content of Epiphany itself understood to be the celebration of the baptism of Jesus in the Jordan, has early precedent in the West as well as in the East. Whatever may have been the case in the earliest Syrian and Egyptian traditions, baptism at Epiphany is documented not only among the Cappadocian Fathers in the late fourth century but also for Spain (together with Christmas and the feasts of apostles and martyrs), Sicily, and possibly north Italy, although for north Italy all that is certain is that the baptism of Jesus was a primary focus of the feast.[50] In addition, an Epiphany vigil, although not clearly baptismal in orientation, appears in the eighth-century Gallican *Missale Gothicum*.[51] Given the overall John 3:5 baptismal emphasis in the Gallican baptismal rites, as we saw above, it is nonetheless quite possible that this vigil represents the trace or remnant of a baptismal custom that was once more pronounced and widespread in this tradition as well.

Futher support for this *may* be provided by attention to the origins of the season of Advent in the West. While much of contemporary scholarship on the evolution of the liturgical year itself has tended to discount previously held theories that claimed that part of the development of the Advent season (often six weeks or forty days in duration), at least in those Western churches outside of Rome, was related to preparation for baptism on Epiphany,[52] Martin Connell has recently argued, quite convincingly, that such scholarly discounting may be rather premature. According to him, the fact that, outside of Rome, Epiphany predates the celebration of Christmas, together with an abundance of references to a forty-day or other period of preparation in early (fourth and fifth century) and later (early medieval) non-Roman liturgical sources, some which include Christmas itself within this reckoning, others which do not, may provide some circumstantial evidence for speculating still that a pre-Epiphany "Advent," with baptismal connotations, may itself also predate the celebration of a December 25 Christmas in those areas of the church. Only when the December 25 feast was adopted, would Advent as we know it ultimately have become limited in focus as a season of preparation for this new feast on the calendar.[53] If Connell is correct in his speculations, an earlier under-standing and orientation may still appear as traces or remnants in the extant sources and, as such, may help in the assessment that outside of Rome Epiphany itself may have often included baptism as part of the celebra-tion of the feast.

Nevertheless, whatever the case may or may not have been historically in the West, for theological reasons the Epiphany baptismal vigil model proposed in the *Episcopal Book of Occasional Services* may well be worth wider ecu-menical adaptation and exploration. While in the Roman Rite catechumens and candidates preparing for Easter initiation are today often accepted into the catechumenal process on the First Sunday of Advent already (although this is neither required nor suggested by the text itself), is there any reason why the Roman RCIA itself could not be adapted to an Epiphany-based model with the rite of election, rather than acceptance, taking place on the first Sunday of Advent and with baptism and other rites of initiation then celebrated on the eve of the Sunday after the Epiphany in the context of a similar vigil? An adap-tation of the rite of election, also including scrutinies on the Second, Third and Fourth Sundays of Advent, are, in fact, provided for both in the Episcopal *Book of Occasional Services*[54] as well as in some recent Lutheran adaptations of the catechumenal process.[55]

Again, whatever its precise origins, the Advent season itself today does provide a rather extensive liturgical-catechetical "textbook" for baptismal catechesis and mystagogy, with John the Baptizer himself, and, hence, Jordan imagery, appearing in the gospel readings on the Second and Third Sundays of Advent in all three cycles of the lectionary. Not only is the overall eschatological orientation of Advent itself easily compatible with a baptismal focus, but the second reading for the Christmas "Mass at Dawn" is precisely Titus 3:4–7, where baptism as regeneration through the Holy Spirit is proclaimed (recall Pope Leo I's Christmas homily quoted above), the second reading for January 1, the Solemnity of Mary, Mother of God, is Galatians 4:4–7, where the baptismal Spirit of adoption enabling us to call God "Abba, Father," is highlighted, and the second reading for the Second Sunday after Christmas is Ephesians 1:3–6, 15–18, where, again, our (baptismal?) adoption and illumination in Christ is the focus, providing an additional baptismal-catechetical emphasis. Together with the juxtaposition of John the Baptizer and Christ in the Prologue of John's gospel (John 1:1–18) read both for the Christmas "Mass During the Day" and again on the Second Sunday after Christmas, a potential baptismal theme or focus from the First Sunday of Advent all the way through the celebration of the Baptism of our Lord is already present within the liturgy itself.

The recovery of such a focus, together with baptisms on the Sunday after the Epiphany within the context of a vigil on the evening before, might not only assist us in our baptismal catechesis and celebration but may actually provide a way for us to re-think the meaning of Advent itself as something beyond Christmas shopping and, hence, assist us in preparing the way for appropriating Christmas as the celebration of what the late New Testament scholar Raymond Brown called "an adult Christ at Christmas."[56] For, after all, the Christ who is "born" at Christmas is, in reality, already, always and forever the adult crucified and risen Christ who seeks to be "reborn" in people by baptism through water and the Holy Spirit. Perhaps the feast of Christmas itself is little more than a joyful pause and celebration on the way to Epiphany (or, in our current tradition, to the Sunday after the Epiphany). In other words, perhaps Christmas is little more than a dramatic preview of the status, privilege, illumination, dignity and adoption that awaits all some twelve days later as new children of God in the Incarnate Son of God himself, revealed by the descending dove of the Spirit and divine voice in the water-filled womb of the Jordan. Perhaps it is not really Christmas but the feast of Jesus' baptism where Advent itself is directed in its call to "prepare the way." And, perhaps, then, Advent itself is best understood as a season of pregnancy not in terms of Christ's birth in Bethlehem but in terms of a catechumenal pregnancy in the womb of the church.

Finally, in spite of the fact that this image is often neglected or relegated to a lesser place in our baptismal celebration, catechesis and mystagogy, one place where it is present is in the prayer of dedication of the baptismal font in the Roman *Rite of Dedication of a Church:*

> Here is reflected the mystery of the church.
> The church is fruitful,
> Made holy by the blood of Christ:
> a bride made radiant with his glory,
> a virgin splendid in the wholeness of her faith,
> a mother blessed through the power of the Spirit.[57]

Consequently, together with a recovery of Epiphany-related baptism itself, the appropriation of this rich image of new birth and adoption, together with its maternal, life-giving and reproductive associations for both the Holy Spirit and the church, might also be assisted by attention to the very shape of baptismal fonts or pools in our worship spaces. If the now popular six-sided, cruciform or tomb-like shapes of fonts or pools readily suggest a Romans 6 paschal interpretation of baptism, surely circular or womb-like baptismal fonts or pools can assist us in the re-appropriation of this equally powerful Epiphany-Incarnational image. In her book on baptismal fonts, Regina Kuehn writes:

> The word "womb" connotes a warm, cavernous, sheltering place where something can grow, develop to capacity and then be born into a new way of life. We speak of the "womb of time" where ideas are conceived and then develop. A mother's womb is the primordial place in which each off-spring receives its initial imprint and pattern, influencing and, to some extent, determining its course for life. . . . Christians have long given some of their baptismal fonts the shape and the quality of a womb. In such fonts the mystery of faith is revealed by the very shape of the vessel containing the life-giving water. Perhaps it is the font's water, one with the life-sustaining waters of earth and the mothering waters of the womb, that makes the metaphor of the womb an appropriate way to understand the church's baptismal font, whether the external shape suggests it or not. Surely we glimpse here a powerful image of our tradition.[58]

As we have seen throughout this chapter, such a focus does, indeed, help us glimpse an often neglected but "powerful image of our tradition." Even if something like the RCIA in its fullness cannot, for some reason, be implemented within the context of an Advent-to-Epiphany catechumenal period, surely the feast of the Baptism of our Lord suggests itself as a prime occasion, at least, for the full, public and communal celebration of infant baptism, and for various rites of baptismal affirmation or renewal together with greater use of *asperges* (sprinkling) rites for the whole liturgical assembly. The Byzantine custom of blessing homes with blessed water around the time of Epiphany is a custom not only well worth our emulation but is also not far removed from the blessing of homes at Epiphany under the initials CMB (*Christus mansem benedicat,* "May Christ bless this home" or, on a popular level, the names of the Magi, Caspar, Melchior, Balthsar), once quite common in the West as well. For, like Easter itself, certainly the feast of

Jesus' baptism is best understood and celebrated as a feast of our baptismal identity, of who God has made us to be through water and the Holy Spirit in the watery womb of the font!

Conclusion

In attempting to explain why it was that Romans 6, rather than John 3 or the related paradigm of Jesus' baptism, became *the* baptismal image of choice for the church in the late fourth-century Kilian McDonnell has recently suggested that in order

> to accommodate [the] new flood of converts, some may have thought that Romans 6:4 offered possibilities the Jordan event did not. For all—Jews, Gentiles, catechumens, Christians—death is a more primary anthropological event, a weightier universal experience, more threatening, rooted deep in the archaeology of dread, tapping unconscious forces of great power. In symbol, drama and imagination, it makes the Jordan event seem almost decorative. The pastoral and liturgical possibilities of death and resurrection, together with the call to radical conversion implicit in it, may have been too much to resist.[59]

I suspect that McDonnell is basically correct in his conjecture, especially within the overall patriarchal context of both church and society in the late fourth and early fifth centuries. But I suspect, further, that women, especially those who have experienced childbirth and motherhood, might well question whether pregnancy and giving birth are not equally primary anthropological events, equally weighty and threatening experiences, which tap unconscious forces of great power. Certainly the experience of giving life is as profound as the experience of death. Indeed, in a time period such as our own when we are intent on rescuing and affirming the human and diverse values, experiences, and contributions of all who make up the church, certainly the strong feminine associations with this baptismal image are worth highlighting and underscoring strongly.

In saying this, however, I do not mean to imply that baptism as death, burial and resurrection is somehow only a masculine baptismal image and that new birth and adoption images are only feminine. All who are baptized are plunged into Christ's death, burial and resurrection, and all simultaneously come to new birth, adoption and new life in the womb of the baptismal font through the mothering Spirit of God in the context of Mother Church. But this particular image, together with womb-like fonts themselves, does invite reflection and critique on the way in which baptism is often taught and celebrated. And, although motherhood should by no means be viewed as the defining characteristic or experience of the identity of women, baptism as new birth and adoption certainly does provide one way in which some feminine imagery for baptism, for the identity of the church and even for how we understand the life-giving role of the Holy Spirit in the church might begin to enter more deeply into our baptismal consciousness. Even with regard to prebaptismal catechesis, both of adults and of parents of infant candidates, catechists might well consider inviting representative parents from their local faith communities, both biological and adoptive parents, who can articulate clearly their own experiences of life-giving, pregnancy, birth and nurture and what it means for them to be parents in a Christian context. Adoptive parents, especially, might provide solid catechesis about the gift and challenge of baptismal adoption into this network of divine and human relationships called church. As Mark Searle noted:

> The events of conception, pregnancy, birth, and parenthood, read in faith, evoke in turn the priestly function of the domestic church; a priesthood exercised in thanksgiving and intercession certainly but also in the rituals and "sacraments" of family

life which include everything from prenatal diet and exercise to the most mundane aspects of caring for the newborn.[60]

Here as well, catechesis for godparents, privileged to act themselves as "midwives" both in baptism and in subsequent Christian nurture, might well focus on this image as well. And, of course, mystagogically, the parental-mothering role of the entire faith community may well be fostered more consciously by greater attention to this image. A dear friend of mine, a Greek Orthodox Christian, likes to say that within any church he enters, he knows that every elderly woman and man is somehow his grandmother and grandfather, and everyone else is part of his extended family. That is the kind of baptismal-ecclesiological consciousness that might be formed by attention to the common womb of the font from which all Christian life comes.

Sometimes it is suggested that Romans 6 is a more appropriate image for the baptism of adults who have consciously converted to Christ and have consciously died to a former way of life to do so, and that, by comparison, John 3 is, thus, a more appropriate image for the baptism of infants and younger children. But if this image of new birth and adoption does lend itself well to the baptism of infants in ways that death, burial and resurrection do not do so as readily, it would be incorrect to try to maintain these two sets of images exclusively, that is, to maintain Romans 6 for adult baptism and John 3 for infant baptism alone. Similarly, while it might be relatively easy in our current situation to make the feast of Jesus' baptism on the Sunday after the Epiphany a prime occasion for the celebration of infant baptism and to emphasize adult baptism at the Easter Vigil, such would not be a pastorally or catechetically helpful way to go. Again, as Mark Searle wrote:

> [B]oth sets of images are properly activated in any baptism, which means that adult initiation needs to be thought of in terms of rebirth and return to infancy, while infants, if they

are to be baptized, must be capable in some way of dying and rising with Christ.[61]

All who are baptized into Christ are baptized into his death, burial and resurrection, just as all who are baptized into Christ, infants and adults, become newly born members of Christ, "neophytes," or, to use the language of our classic liturgical texts, *"infantes"* (infants) themselves. Hence, infant baptism belongs to the Easter Vigil and its theology of Romans 6, and adult baptism belongs to the Jordan event and its theology of John 3 celebrated annually on the feast of Jesus' baptism by John.

Indeed, baptism as new birth or adoption through water and the Holy Spirit is part of our ancient, common and ecumenical liturgical heritage of the church, both East and West, and, in my opinion, we would do well today to recover, pay renewed attention to and underscore that common heritage strongly. Without attention to this equally dominant image in our baptismal-liturgical traditions our baptismal catechesis, mystagogy and celebration become far less rich than they could be.

Chapter 3

Baptism as the Sacrament and Seal of the Holy Spirit

■

In him you also, when you had heard the word of truth, the gospel of your salvation and had believed in him, were marked with the seal of the promised Holy Spirit; this is the pledge of our inheritance toward redemption as God's own people, to the praise of his glory. (Ephesians 1:13–14)

When it was evening on that day; the first day of the week and the doors of the house where the disciples had met were locked for fear of the Jews, Jesus came and stood among them and said, "Peace be with you." After he said this, he showed them his hands and his side. Then the disciples rejoiced when they saw the Lord. Jesus said to them again, "Peace be with you. As the Father has sent me, so I send you." When he had said this, he breathed on them and said to them, "Recieve the Holy Spirit. If you forgive the sins of any, they are forgiven them; if you retain the sins of any, they are retained." (John 20:19–23)

Of the biblical texts quoted above, there is probably no better one than John 20:19–23 to show the inseparable and unitive nature of Jesus' death, resurrection and gift of the Holy Spirit as the one great and single mystery of our Christian faith. Here on Easter Sunday, the risen Christ, who by the wounds in his hands, feet and side, shows himself to be the Crucified One, breathes the Holy Spirit into the church, just as God had breathed life into Adam at creation and sends the church on its mission of reconciliation and forgiveness in the world. Sunday, cross, resurrection, Spirit, mission—this text from John 20 brings together Good Friday, Easter Sunday and Pentecost, all rooted in the mystery of God, who according to John, had sent the Son himself into the world that "all who believe in him might not perish but have eternal life," and "that the world might be saved through him" (John 3).

It is this unity of the trinitarian mystery of God, the inseparable oneness and threefold saving activity of Father, Son and Holy Spirit, that is central to any discussion of liturgy and sacraments, especially the rites of Christian initiation. We call this mystery, of course, the Paschal Mystery, but we should be careful and clear in our use of this term. The term "Paschal Mystery" I fear, is becoming little more than a cliché, frequently invoked in our day as a catch-all for any and everything Christian, and a term usually limited in focus to Jesus' dying and rising alone. As this text from John makes clear, however, what we call the Paschal Mystery is never *only* Jesus' death and resurrection or our own baptismal deaths and resurrections in him. It is also the very presence, activity and breath of the Holy Spirit among us, who if not limited to the proclamation of the word and celebration of the sacraments, is at least bound to them for our sake for life and salvation. Without the Holy Spirit, the word isn't the word, baptism not baptism, confirmation not confirmation, and eucharist not the eucharist. Indeed, it is the Holy Spirit, the very breath of God in us, who conforms us to the dying and rising of Christ in our lives, who brings us to new birth and regenerates us to new life in the living waters and womb of the font, who seals us in down payment for redemption, who gives us special charisms and gifts for the building up of and living within Christ's body, the church, the Spirit of God who directs us in our mission of reconciling love, forgiveness and justice in the world, the Spirit alone who makes it possible for us to say, "We believe" or "I believe" in the first place. Whatever baptismal image or metaphor might be dominant, all of them include, inseparably, the Holy Spirit. We dare not forget this. Faith itself is a gift of the Holy Spirit breathing among us. Here are together cross, resurrection, Spirit, mission, faith, the Sunday gathering of the church and the love and grace of God, which makes it all possible in the first place. If we wish to keep using the terminology of "Paschal Mystery," we dare not narrow it from its unitive and biblical fullness.

The Second Vatican Council, in the words of Pope John XXIII, was a call for a new Pentecost, a new outpouring of the Holy Spirit in the church in order that the breath of God's Spirit might bring about an *aggiornamento,* fresh air, a new time of renewal and hope. Such a new Pentecost of renewal and change, of course, was and continues to be needed, especially in relationship to the role of and attention to the Holy Spirit in the church. We Western Christians, Catholic and Protestant alike, have not always done a very good job in articulating the central, necessary and unitive role of the Holy Spirit either in the church, in our lives or within the sacramental, Spirit-bound, liturgical rites of the church. Due in part to that weak pneumatology, or minimal emphasis on the Holy Spirit, for example, our Western tradition tends even to separate the Spirit from baptism almost entirely, with the result that, at least in the popular imagination and far too often in practice, baptism itself, especially infant baptism, has been seen by us as little more than a solemn "operation on the child,"[1] a solemn exorcism designed to rid the child from his or her inherited original sin, or, given its close association to birth, a naming ceremony for the child ("christening").

With this strange separation of the Spirit from baptism, we in the West, due to a variety of interesting historical, political and ecclesiastical shifts, ended up by creating a distinct sacramental rite altogether for celebrating what is nothing other than, in its complicated origins, the baptismal gift of that Spirit in Christian initiation. This rite, of course, is confirmation, a rite often separated from baptism by several years with the result that in the Roman Catholic dioceses of the United States today, the normative age for confirmation varies from age 7—still the canonical "age of reason"—all the way to age 18. But if in the Roman Rite confirmation celebrates the *initiatory* gift of the Holy Spirit, then, doesn't this Holy Spirit gift remain intimately connected with baptism itself? The Fathers of the church certainly thought so and would be quite perplexed if they knew our current practice. Indeed, if the gift of the Spirit is tied to baptism, why is it that to receive this gift one must wait for the baptismal seal of the Spirit until one is old enough, presumably 7 to 18 years later, to understand and be catechized on the meaning of the Holy Spirit? A catechetical rite in adolescence celebrating one's affirmation of faith or adult commitment, an affirmation rite, for example, as currently celebrated in a variety of Protestant traditions, is one thing. To call that rite "confirmation," and to relate it explicitly to the baptismal seal of the Holy Spirit at age 7 or above, for those already baptized in infancy, is quite another.

With regard to the separation of the Holy Spirit from the eucharist, we in the West traditionally have ended up with a rather narrow theology focused on a Real Presence confected by the words of Jesus alone without much attention given to the role of the Holy Spirit or, for that matter, to the whole prayer and invocation of the church gathered around the Lord's altar. Indeed, from the time of Ambrose of Milan in the late fourth century until the publication of the new eucharistic prayers in the current Missal of Pope Paul VI (1969), the only eucharistic prayer used in the Roman Rite, the Roman *canon missae* (now called Eucharistic Prayer I), did not even so much as mention the Holy Spirit until the final doxology

("Through him, with him, in him, in the unity of the Holy Spirit . . . "). With such a traditional lack of emphasis on the Spirit in the eucharist, it is not surprising that few today have any real conception that the eucharist too is about the gift and activity of the Holy Spirit, that the Spirit is not only involved in bringing the words and promise of Jesus to life among us here and now, but that part of the very meaning of receiving communion is what the New Testament calls the *koinonia,* or "communion of the Holy Spirit," which is established in the church by sharing the bread and cup with another. It is this we now actually evoke at the beginning of the eucharistic rite itself: "The grace of our Lord Jesus Christ, the love of God and the fellowship [*koinonia,* communion] of the Holy Spirit be with you all."

It is no wonder then that, according to Roman Catholic teaching, eucharistic participation—not confirmation—is both the completion and fullness of Christian initiation. For one cannot become more fully initiated into Christ and his body the church than by sharing in his body and blood. But even this is not always clearly signified or understood in either traditional or contemporary Western, especially Roman Catholic, practice where, again, for those baptized in infancy, first eucharist, the very completion of Christian initiation, often comes before confirmation, depending on diocese, or where, even in a more obviously contradictory manner, first reconciliation with the church comes even before one is fully initiated into the very community with whom one seeks reconciliation.

This traditional but unfortunate Western separation of the Holy Spirit from the rites of Christian initiation was addressed clearly in the reform of the initiation rites called for at the Second Vatican Council. In the *Rite of Christian Initiation of Adults,* considered by many to be the most mature of Vatican II's liturgical reforms, the following statement appears:

> The [necessary] conjunction of the two celebrations [baptism and confirmation] signifies the unity of the paschal mystery, the close link between the mission of the Son and the outpouring of the Holy Spirit and the connection between the two sacraments through which the Son and the Holy Spirit come with the Father to those who are baptized.[2]

While this statement itself clearly underscores the unitive and inseparable connection between baptism and confirmation in the current Roman Rite, this chapter is about baptism itself as the sacrament or "seal" of the Holy Spirit. In what follows, I wish to highlight and underscore how the rite of baptism itself already points to the inseparable presence and activity of the Holy Spirit. I shall do this both by paying attention to those lectionary readings assigned to the Roman *Rite for the Baptism of Children,* where the relationship of the Holy Spirit to baptism is central, and to the language of the rite itself. Second, I will address some issues related to the Holy Spirit in the eucharistic liturgy and communion, especially as they pertain to initiation. And, finally, I will relate this baptismal image to the feast of Pentecost and make some suggestions with regard to Pentecost as an especially significant occasion for the celebration of baptism.

The Holy Spirit and Baptism

Baptism as New Birth in Water and the Holy Spirit (Mark 1:9–11; John 3:1–6)

It is rather unfortunate that a reading from Titus 3 (i.e., "[God] saved us . . . through the water of rebirth and renewal by the Holy Spirit," Titus 3:5) is not included in the lectionary provided in the Roman *Rite of Baptism for Children.* Nevertheless, reading as the gospel either the account of Jesus' own baptism in the Jordan (Mark 1:9–11) or the conversation between Jesus and Nicodemus regarding the necessity of "being begotten of water and Spirit" (John 3:1–6) brings into focus the particularly rich image of baptism as a new birth or adoption through water and the Holy Spirit, which I addressed in detail in the previous chapter. I note it here again in this chapter simply because this image, of course, is precisely about the role of the Holy Spirit in baptism. For, after all, it is the Holy Spirit who is the primary actor in this baptismal new birth and adoption, an understanding that has given baptism a precise pneumatological focus throughout the history of the church, even if often ignored. Hence, to pay attention to the baptismal image of new birth and adoption, of course, is already to attend as well to baptism as the sacrament or seal of the Holy Spirit, a focus highlighted for centuries in the West by means of the (first) postbaptismal anointing prayer, which has always referred explicitly to John 3:5 or Titus 3:5. "Water baptism" and "Spirit baptism" have always gone together in the Christian sacramental economy, even if the connection, due to confirmation, has not always been clear. Indeed, Christian baptism is baptism in water and the Holy Spirit. Without the Holy Spirit baptism is not baptism.

Such an integral and necessary connection between baptism and the Holy Spirit is central to how modern biblical scholarship often interprets those passages in the Acts of the Apostles, especially Acts 8:14–17 and Acts 19:1–7, where it appears that in addition to baptism itself another rite of handlaying was needed in order to bestow the gift of the Spirit to those who had already been baptized. Acts 8:14–17, for example, tells of certain Samaritan converts who, having received baptism "in the name of the Lord Jesus," had not received the Holy Spirit. Only when the apostles Peter and John laid hands on them and prayed for the Holy Spirit did that Spirit finally come to them. Similarly, in Acts 19:1–7 we read of twelve disciples in Ephesus who had not received (or even heard of) the Holy Spirit but had been baptized only with John the Baptizer's "baptism of repentance." In response to

Paul, they are baptized "in the name of the Lord Jesus," and then, through the laying on of Paul's hands, they too receive the Holy Spirit.

Most New Testament scholars today would find reading something like a rite of confirmation into these texts to be anachronistic, that is, reading back into the New Testament a ritual pattern known only on the basis of later practice. Alternatively, scholars have underscored the apparent exceptional and rather unique contexts and situations of both of these texts. The event described in Acts 8 is concerned with the conversion and initiation of *Samaritans,* whose conversion and initiation came about not by or under the direction of the Jerusalem apostles, but through the mission of Philip. Along similar lines, the context and situation in Acts 19:1–7 concerns those who had received only *John's* baptism, not *Christian* baptism; it is Christian baptism alone which gives the Holy Spirit. *That* appears to be the point precisely in these texts! Such situations as these, then, can hardly be seen as reflecting some sort of normative liturgical pattern or theology, but, rather, they are specific and unique occasions, brought about by specific, unique and irregular situations.[3] In fact, what these two texts seem to be underscoring, as certainly the baptismal theology of Paul himself does throughout his letters, is that baptism and the Holy Spirit always go together inseparably! As such, those situations described in Acts 8 and 19 were those which for some reason had departed from that norm and so had to be dealt with in an extraordinary manner.

Christian baptism is simply *not* the baptism of John theologically or sacramentally. According to John the Baptizer's own words: "I have baptized you with water; but he will baptize you with the Holy Spirit" (Mark 1:8). And it is the presence and gift of the Holy Spirit that makes all the difference in the world in terms of baptism's meaning and significance. Christian baptism is baptism "with the Holy Spirit!"

Baptism as the Sacrament of the Holy Spirit (Ezekiel 36:24–28; 1 Corinthians 12:12–13; Matthew 28:18–20; John 7:37–39) In close relationship to the image of baptism as new birth in water and the Holy Spirit, other examples are available to demonstrate this necessary connection between the gift of the Holy Spirit and baptism itself. Such a biblical emphasis, underscored even by the formula of "Father, Son and *Holy Spirit*" used in the very administration of baptism, is of great importance in understanding and proclaiming the overall meaning of this life-giving sacrament.

On the basis of the separated and out of sequence sacramental pattern of the full rites of Christian initiation as they are celebrated with children, however and now especially with the use of "Be sealed with the gift of the Holy Spirit" as the formula for confirmation in the Roman Rite, the impression is given far too often that baptism itself has to do only with a preliminary absolution or removal of original sin and that the "real" gift of the Holy Spirit is reserved for confirmation at a later point in the candidate's life. By focusing on *baptism* as the sacrament of the Holy Spirit, then, we have the great opportunity here to address what has often been an inadequate and minimalist understanding of baptism in our Western tradition. Here we would do well to review what the General Introduction to Christian Initiation says about the relation between baptism and the Holy Spirit:

> Baptism is . . . , above all, the sacrament of that faith by which, *enlightened by the grace of the Holy Spirit,* we respond to the Gospel of Christ. . . .
>
> . . . Further, baptism is the sacrament by which its recipients are incorporated into the church and are built up together *in the Spirit* into a house where God lives, into a holy and royal priesthood. . . .
>
> . . . Baptism, the cleansing with water by the power of the living word, washes away every stain of sin, original and personal and makes us sharers in God's own life and his adopted children. As proclaimed in the prayers for the blessing of the

water, baptism is a cleansing water of rebirth that makes us God's children born from on high. The blessed Trinity is invoked over those who are to be baptized, so that all who are signed in this name are consecrated to the Trinity and *enter into communion with the Father, the Son and the Holy Spirit.*[4]

Helpful as well on this issue is the following statement in the World Council of Churches' ecumenical convergence document, *Baptism, Eucharist and Ministry:*

> The Holy Spirit is at work in the lives of people before, in and after their baptism. It is the same Spirit who revealed Jesus as the Son (Mark 1:10–11) and who empowered and united the disciples at Pentecost (Acts 2). God bestows upon all baptized persons the anointing and promise of the Holy Spirit, marks them with a seal and implants in their hearts the first install-ment of their inheritance as sons and daughters of God. The Holy Spirit nurtures the life of faith in their hearts until the final deliverance when they will enter into its full possession, to the praise of the glory of God (2 Corinthians 1:21–22; Ephesians 1:13–14).[5]

While confirmation as a special celebration of the gift and role of the Holy Spirit in Christian life may play a particular role in the development and catechetical for-mation of those baptized in infancy, those who prepare parents, godparents and communities for the celebration of the baptism of children have the opportunity to under-score the importance and implications of that Spirit's gift and role at the very sacramental *inception* of one's life in Christ. Here, especially, we might note that all life in Christ is dependent upon the presence and guidance of the Holy Spirit. It is, after all, the Holy Spirit who is active in the baptismal plunge into the Paschal Mystery of Christ's death and resurrection, the Holy Spirit who brings about that new birth "from above" in the waters of baptism, and the Holy Spirit who makes all faith in God possible. The Holy Spirit can no more be separated from the sacrament of baptism than from the mystery of the Trinity itself. Again, without the Holy Spirit baptism

82   is not baptism!

That the Holy Spirit is directly involved throughout the entire celebration of baptism is abundantly clear from the texts of the rite itself. Even in a prebaptismal context the first option for the "Prayer of Exorcism and Anointing before Baptism" in the Roman *Rite of Baptism for Children* refers explicitly to a giving of the Spirit:"We pray for these children: set them free from original sin, make them temples of your glory and *send your Holy Spirit to dwell within them*."[6] As we have seen before, the prayer for the blessing of the waters connects this gift of the Holy Spirit to the image of baptismal participation in Christ's death and resurrection: "We ask you, Father, with your Son to send the Holy Spirit upon the waters of this font. May all who are buried with Christ in the death of baptism rise also with him to newness of life."[7] And, as we saw in detail in the previous chapter, the formula for the postbaptismal anointing likewise connects the gift of the Spirit to the baptismal washing itself:

> The God of power . . . has freed you from sin and brought you to new life through water and *the Holy Spirit*. He now anoints you with the chrism of salvation, so that, united with his people, you may remain forever a member of Christ who is Priest, prophet and king.

That's what the Holy Spirit does in baptism, a gift expressed even more strongly and explicitly in the case of adult initiation, where, in the Roman Rite, the confirmation prayer for the sevenfold gift of the Holy Spirit and the chrismation and seal of the Holy Spirit follow baptism immediately in place of this anointing:

> 234. The celebrant holds his hands outstretched over the entire group of those to be confirmed and says the following prayer.
>
> [In silence the priests associated as ministers of the sacrament also hold their hands outstretched over the candidates.]
>
> All—powerful God, Father of our Lord Jesus Christ, by water and the Holy Spirit you freed your sons and daughters from sin and gave them new life.

Send your Holy Spirit upon them to be their helper and guide.

Give them the spirit of wisdom and understanding, the spirit of right judgment and courage, the spirit of knowledge and reverence. Fill them with the spirit of wonder and awe in your presence.

We ask this through Christ our Lord.
R. Amen.

ANOINTING WITH CHRISM

235. A minister brings the chrism to the celebrant. . . .

Each candidate, with godparent or godparents, goes to the celebrant (or to an associated minister of the sacrament); or, if circumstances require, the celebrant (associated ministers) may go to the candidates.

Either or both godparents place the right hand on the shoulder of the candidate and either a godparent or the candidate gives the candidate's name to the minister of the sacrament. During the conferral of the sacrament a suitable song may be sung.

The minister of the sacrament dips his right thumb in the chrism and makes the sign of the cross on the forehead of the one to be confirmed as he says:

N., be sealed with the Gift of the Holy Spirit.

Newly confirmed:
Amen.

The minister of the sacrament adds:
Peace be with you.

Newly confirmed:
Amen.[8]

It may be helpful in this context to look at the post-baptismal rites associated with the gift of the Holy Spirit in some other liturgical traditions as well. Within the 1979 *Book of Common Prayer* of the Episcopal Church, USA, for example, the following unit appears not as confirmation but as the regular postbaptismal rite:

> *When [Baptism] has been completed for all candidates, the Bishop or Priest, at a place in full sight of the congregation, prays over them, saying*

Let us pray.

Heavenly Father, we thank you that by water and the Holy Spirit you have bestowed upon *these* your *servants* the forgiveness of sin and have raised *them* to the new life of grace. Sustain *them,* O Lord, in your Holy Spirit. Give *them* an inquiring and discerning heart, the courage to will and to persevere, a spirit to know and to love you and the gift of joy and wonder in all your works. Amen.

Then the Bishop or Priest places a hand on the person's head, marking on the forehead the sign of the cross [using Chrism if desired] and saying to each one

N., you are sealed by the Holy Spirit in Baptism and marked as Christ's own for ever. Amen.[9]

Similarly, the following regular postbaptismal rite appears in the *Lutheran Book of Worship* of the Evangelical Lutheran church in America (ELCA):

. . . The minister lays both hands on the head of each of the baptized and prays for the Holy Spirit:

P. God, the Father of our Lord Jesus Christ, we give you thanks for freeing your sons and daughters from the power of sin and for raising them up to a new life through this holy sacrament. Pour your Holy Spirit upon ___name___: the spirit of wisdom and understanding, the spirit of counsel and might, the spirit of knowledge and the fear of the Lord, the spirit of joy in your presence.

C. Amen.

The minister marks the sign of the cross on the forehead of each of the baptized. Oil prepared for this purpose may be used. As the sign of the cross is made, the minister says:

P. ___name___, child of God, you have been sealed by the Holy Spirit and marked with the cross of Christ forever.

The sponsor or the baptized responds: 'Amen.'[10]

It must be noted that, whereas the confirmation prayer for the sevenfold gift of the Holy Spirit and the anointing with the seal of the Holy Spirit appear in such close relationship to baptism in the Roman Rite only when adults are being initiated, both the Episcopal and Lutheran postbaptismal rites are for all baptismal candidates, infants, children and adults alike. That is, what the RCIA has done for adult initiation in the Roman Catholic Church in restoring confirmation to baptism, the rites of other churches, including not only those of Episcopalians and (at least ELCA) Lutherans but those of several other Protestant traditions as well (e.g., Presbyterian and United Methodist), have done for baptism in all cases. In other words, all who are baptized according to these rites are likewise "sealed" by the sevenfold gift of the Holy Spirit. While some may understand this postbaptismal unit as the equivalent to the postbaptismal "explanatory rites" of the Roman baptismal rite, underscoring, highlighting and ritualizing the Spirit-gift bestowed *in* baptism, Roman Catholics cannot fail to recognize that this unit, including the possibility of the use of chrism, is nothing other than the ritual and liturgical equivalent to confirmation in the Roman Rite. Hence, from a Roman Catholic theological perspective, at least, there is no question but that Episcopalians and Lutherans (and others) are actually "confirming" infants at their baptism with a language and ritual closely parallel to Roman Catholic confirmation, much as has always been the case within the unbroken baptismal traditions of the Christian East.

This not only speaks volumes about the necessary and integral connection between Christian baptism and the gift of the Holy Spirit in general, but it also has some serious and profound ecumenical implications about what is to be done ritually and/or sacramentally when receiving Christians, who are already baptized according to the rites of other traditions, into full communion. Especially with regard to the reception of already baptized Christians into full communion with the Roman Catholic Church, what is being said both theologically and sacramentally when confirmation, the very equivalent to the postbaptismal prayer for the sevenfold gift and sealing of the Holy Spirit, is repeated? Are not Protestants sealed with the Holy Spirit in baptism as these rites attest?

Is "Protestant" baptism in water *and the Holy Spirit* really only the equivalent of John's baptism which, as in Acts 19:1–7, necessitates some kind of apostolic ratification and completion? Tradition-specific catechesis and formation is one thing and is to be expected and encouraged, as is, of course, some celebratory rite of reception for those who seek to live out their baptismal identity in a particular ecclesial manner of baptismal life. But to repeat an equivalent but mandatory rite is something altogether different and may say something even about the ecumenical perception and acceptance of the fullness of baptism in other traditions itself. Here I can only echo the words of Roman Catholic liturgist Paul Turner:

> The ecumenical movement longs for the day when the rites which prepare baptized Christians for full communion will be ripped from our books and the catechumenate now so freely adapted for the *baptized* may become again the proper province of the unbaptized. . . . When the disciples warned Jesus that some who were not of their company were exorcising demons in his name they expected him to put a stop to it. Jesus tolerated strange exorcists with the simplest of aphorisms: "If they're not against us, they're for us." The church tolerates baptisms. Is it too much to ask that we tolerate confirmations as well? Our churches are irresponsibly dawdling toward a common table.[11]

Indeed, *is* it too much to ask, especially when the language, ritual actions and sacramental signs of the Roman rite of confirmation itself are precisely those present in the inseparably connected postbaptismal rites associated with the Holy Spirit in the very baptismal rites of so many other Christian traditions today? Or do these other baptismal rites in water and the Holy Spirit not really mean and effect what they signify?

The Holy Spirit and the Adult Catechumenate Much of what I have been saying so far has dealt most directly with issues related to the baptism of infants. Let me suggest that such emphases are equally important and just as necessary when dealing with the RCIA or other adaptations of the adult catechumenal process underway in other churches today. In the concluding chapter of my recent book, *The Rites of Christian Initiation: Their Evolution and Interpretation* (Collegeville: The Liturgical Press, 1999), I argued that the churches, perhaps today more than ever, are called to a renewed stance against that sort of creeping Pelagianism which affects much of what today is generically called "spirituality" in especially an American context. Pelagianism was the ancient North African heresy, fought against by Augustine of Hippo and others, which taught that humans were born free and neutral, could choose for themselves whether or not to accept God and did not need God's grace in order to make that choice. If that sounds like a rather modern understanding of the relationship between God and human beings, it's probably because many moderns, including many Christians, are Pelagian in their basic outlook and theology. But God's gracious initiative, concretized and mediated as sheer *gift* in the font and in the assembly around the eucharistic table, should give us a firm basis from which to critique and shun this approach. Indeed, a clear baptismal spirituality places the emphasis where it should be: on God, the great author and initiator of salvation.

Such an emphasis calls us to be careful with how the rites of initiation, especially those for adults, are celebrated and presented catechetically today. Designed primarily for missionary contexts, with the initiation of *unbaptized* adults in mind—and not the confirmation of Protestants being received into full communion with the Roman Catholic Church at the Easter Vigil, which, by the way, actually goes against the norms of the National Statutes on the Catechumenate[12]—the RCIA is not a program but a sacramental *process* designed to seal conversion to Christ and the church. But, let's be clear on conversion itself: A conversion is always rooted in the prior activity of the Holy Spirit. Adults need to understand that in

order to make proper theological sense out of their conversion experience. Again, the introduction to the RCIA
says in this context:

> The rite of Christian initiation presented here is designed for
> adults who, *after hearing the mystery of Christ proclaimed,* con-
> sciously and freely seek the living God and enter the way of
> faith and conversion *as the Holy Spirit opens their hearts. By
> God's help* they will be strengthened spiritually during their
> preparation and at the proper time will receive the sacraments
> fruitfully.[13]

Also, note the following statement in the World Council
of Churches' ecumenical convergence document,
Baptism, Eucharist, Ministry:

> The Holy Spirit is at work in the lives of people before, in and
> after their baptism. It is the same Spirit who revealed Jesus as
> the Son (Mark 1:10–11) and who empowered and united the
> disciples at Pentecost (Acts 2). God bestows upon all baptized
> persons the anointing and promise of the Holy Spirit, marks
> them with a seal and implants in their hearts the first install-
> ment of their inheritance as sons and daughters of God. The
> Holy Spirit nurtures the life of faith in their hearts until the
> final deliverance when they will enter into its full possession,
> to the praise of the glory of God (2 Corinthians 1:21–22;
> Ephesians 1:13–14).[14]

The Holy Spirit is active before, in and after baptism.
The introduction to the RCIA couldn't be clearer: Faith
comes how? "After *hearing* the mystery of Christ proclaimed." That is exactly what St. Paul says in Romans
10:17: "So faith comes from what is heard and what is
heard comes through the word of Christ." And how is it
that people "consciously and freely seek God and enter
the way of faith and conversion"? Certainly not by their
own understanding or Pelagian self-sufficiency but only
"by God's help . . . as the Holy Spirit opens their hearts."
We dare not put our emphasis with either children or
adults on what they do or do not do, emphasizing adult
decision, commitment or personal "choice" as the foundation for baptism. Instead we need always to emphasize

the work of the Holy Spirit, God's graciousness, God's own choice made in baptism and the need for all to depend utterly upon the continued presence, guidance and direction of the Holy Spirit. This gracious activity of the Holy Spirit in the word and sacramental life of the faith community always must be stressed. For, after all, it is the Holy Spirit and none other that leads to conversion. It is, says Paul, only in the Holy Spirit that one can confess Jesus as Lord (cf. 1 Corinthians 12:3).

With further regard to the baptismal activity of the Holy Spirit, we would do well to pay close attention to the recently signed Roman Catholic—Lutheran *Joint Declaration on the Doctrine of Justification,* prepared by the Vatican Secretariat for Christian Unity and the Lutheran World Federation. This *Joint Declaration* says in part:

> Together we confess: By grace alone, in faith in Christ's saving work and not because of any merit on our part, we are accepted by God and receive the Holy Spirit, who renews our hearts while equipping and calling us to good works. . . .
>
> . . . Through [Christ] alone are we justified, when we receive this salvation in faith. Faith is itself God's gift through the Holy Spirit who works through Word and Sacrament in the community of believers and who, at the same time, leads believers into that renewal of life which God will bring to completion in eternal life.[15]

And, further:

> . . . [Justification] is more than just one part of Christian doctrine. It stands in an essential relation to all truths of faith, which are to be seen as internally related to each other. It is an indispensable criterion, which constantly serves to orient all the teaching and practice of our churches to Christ.[16]

Perhaps there is no other sacramental act that offers the assembled faith community a more concrete sign that all human salvation is by "grace alone" than does baptism. Again, as the *Joint Declaration* continues:

> (Paragraph 25): We confess together that sinners are justified by faith in the saving action of God in Christ. *By the action of*

the Holy Spirit in baptism, they are granted the gift of salvation, which lays the basis for the whole Christian life. . . . Whatever in the justified precedes or follows the *free gift of faith* is neither the basis of justification nor merits it.[17]

Baptism invites the gathered assembly to faith, trust, dependency and receptivity to the sheer *gift* of God's baptismal grace. The minds and hearts of that assembly are to be continually directed back to the foundational baptismal realities of new birth and new life in the Spirit. Along these lines, there remains more commonality between infant and adult baptism than we may sometimes think. Several years ago Eugene Brand wrote:

> Though a response of faith may antedate Baptism and lead someone to request it, Baptism is largely a prelude to faith, standing, as it does, at the inception of the life in Christ. In regard to faith, almost everyone is baptized in infancy. Baptism has an inescapable proleptic character because it is tied to the future of one's life for its completion.[18]

The Holy Spirit and the Eucharist

In spite of the traditional silence concerning the Holy Spirit in the Roman Canon throughout history, a classic emphasis on the role of the Holy Spirit has been restored in the additional eucharistic prayers in the current *Missal of Pope Paul VI* and in the new eucharistic prayers in the revised worship books of almost every other Christian liturgical tradition today. Such an ecumenical gesture toward the East, where the Holy Spirit's role in the consecration of the bread and cup and the fruits of communion has always been a major emphasis, is probably one of the most significant recoveries of modern eucharistic theology. But what do these texts actually say about the Holy Spirit? In what follows I list several representative eucharistic prayer texts which reflect this emphasis.

Roman Catholic Eucharistic Prayer Texts

Eucharistic Prayer II: Before the words of Christ: "Let your Spirit come upon these gifts to make them holy, so that they may become for us the body and blood of our Lord, Jesus Christ." And at a later point in the prayer: "We thank you for counting us worthy to stand in your presence and serve you. May all of us who share in the body and blood of Christ be brought together in unity by the Holy Spirit."[19]

Eucharistic Prayer III: Before the words of Christ: "And so, Father, we bring you these gifts. We ask you to make them holy by the power of your Spirit that they may become the body and blood of your Son, our Lord Jesus Christ, at whose command we celebrate this Eucharist." And later in the prayer: "Look with favor on your church's offering and see the Victim whose death has reconciled us to yourself. Grant that we, who are nourished by his body and blood, may be filled with his Holy Spirit and become one body, one spirit in Christ."[20]

Eucharistic Prayer IV: Before the words of Christ: "Father, may this Holy Spirit sanctify these offerings. Let them become the body and blood of Jesus Christ our Lord as we celebrate the great mystery which he left us as an everlasting covenant." And later in the prayer: "Lord, look upon this sacrifice which you have given to your church; and by your Holy Spirit, gather all who share this one bread and cup into the one body of Christ, a living sacrifice of praise."[21]

Eucharistic Prayer for Masses of Reconciliation I: Before the words of Christ: "Look with kindness on your people gathered here before you: send forth the power of your Spirit so that these gifts may become for us the body and blood of your beloved Son, Jesus the Christ, in whom we have become your sons and daughters." And later in the prayer: "Father, look with love on those you have called to share in the one sacrifice of Christ. By the power of your Holy Spirit make them one body, healed of all division."[22]

Eucharistic Prayer for Masses of Reconciliation II: Before the words of Christ: "We ask you to sanctify these gifts by the power of your Spirit as we now fulfill your son's command." And later in the prayer: "Fill us with his Spirit through our sharing in this meal. May he take away all that divides us."[23]

Eucharistic Prayer for Masses for Various Needs and Occasions: Before the words of Christ: "Great and merciful Father, we ask you to send down your Holy Spirit to hallow these gifts of bread and wine that they may become for us the body and blood of our Lord Jesus Christ." And later in the prayer: "Look with favor on the offering of your church in which we show forth the paschal sacrifice of Christ entrusted to us. Through the power of your Spirit of love include us now and for ever among the members of your Son whose body and blood we share."[24]

Select Eucharistic Prayer Texts from Other Traditions

Eucharistic Prayer A, Book of Common Prayer: After the anamnesis: "Sanctify them [the bread and cup] by your Holy Spirit to be for your people the Body and Blood of your Son, the holy food and drink of the new and unending life in him. Sanctify us also that we may faithfully receive this holy Sacrament and serve you in unity, constancy and peace; and at the last day bring us with all your saints into the joy of your eternal kingdom."[25]

Eucharistic Prayer B, Book of Common Prayer: After the anamnesis: "We pray you, gracious God, to send your Holy Spirit upon these gifts that they may be the Sacrament of the Body of Christ and his Blood of the new covenant. Unite us to your Son in his sacrifice, that we may be acceptable through him, being sanctified by the Holy Spirit."[26]

Eucharistic Prayer D, Book of Common Prayer: After the anamnesis: "Lord, we pray that in your goodness and mercy your Holy Spirit may descend upon us and upon these gifts, sanctifying them and showing them to be holy gifts for your holy people, the bread of life and the cup of salvation, the Body and Blood of your Son Jesus Christ . . . . Grant that all who share this bread and cup may become one body and one spirit, a living sacrifice in Christ, to the praise of your Name."[27]

Eucharistic Prayer II, Lutheran Book of Worship: After the anamnesis: "Send now, we pray, your Holy Spirit, that we and all who share in this bread and cup may be united in the fellowship of the Holy Spirit, may enter the fullness of the kingdom of heaven and may receive our inheritance with all your saints in light."[28]

Eucharistic Prayer III, Lutheran Book of Worship: After the anamnesis: "we implore you mercifully to accept our praise and thanksgiving and with your Word and Holy Spirit, to bless us your servants and these your own gifts of bread and wine; that we and all who share in the body and blood of your Son may be filled with heavenly peace and joy and receiving the forgiveness of sin, may be sanctified in soul and body and have our portion with all your saints."[29]

Eucharistic Prayer IV, Lutheran Book of Worship: After the anamnesis: "And we ask you: Send your Spirit upon these gifts of your church; gather into one all who share this bread and wine; fill us with your Holy Spirit to establish our faith in truth, that we may praise and glorify you through your Son Jesus Christ."[30]

Such a modern ecumenical move toward the recovery of the Holy Spirit's role in the eucharist has produced such a change of emphasis in Roman Catholic sacramental theology that the recent *Catechism of the Catholic Church* demonstrates a decisive shift away from an overwhelmingly narrow theology of consecration by the words of

Christ alone to say that the eucharist is the presence of Christ: "by the power of his word *and of his Spirit,*"[31] that is, by "the efficacy of the Word of Christ *and* the action of the Holy Spirit" the conversion of the bread and wine into Christ's body and blood are brought about."[32]

More important for our purposes here, however, is the language about the Holy Spirit and the church in the later sections of these eucharistic prayers: "May all of us who share in the body and blood of Christ be brought together in unity by the Holy Spirit"; or "Grant that we, who are nourished by his body and blood, may be filled with his Holy Spirit and become one body, one spirit in Christ"; or "by your Holy Spirit, gather all who share this one bread and cup into the one body of Christ, a living sacrifice of praise"; or "through the power of your Spirit of love include us now and for ever among the members of your Son whose body and blood we share." All of these petitions sound quite similar to what we say baptism itself signifies and gives: receiving the gift of the Holy Spirit, becoming the body of Christ, being made members of Christ and being brought into unity by the gift of the Holy Spirit.

And this is with good reason. Neither baptism nor confirmation are given or received more than once. But the eucharist itself as the fullness and completion of Christian initiation in contemporary Roman Catholic sacramental theology, as the summit to which baptism and confirmation point, is the repeatable sacrament of initiation, which continuously directs us back to baptism itself.

It is no wonder then, as Aidan Kavanagh and others have reminded us in recent years,[33] that the very first use of the word *confirmation* in liturgical history appears not in reference to the bishop's postbaptismal rites of hand-laying and anointing but in relationship to the baptismal eucharist, which culminated and brought to completion the celebration of initiation itself. Indeed, the first reference to the word *confirmation* in relationship to initiation appears in that presumably early-third-century eucharistic prayer from the so-called *Apostolic Tradition,* frequently ascribed to Hippolytus of Rome (ca. 215), which served as the model for Eucharistic Prayer II in the Roman Rite, Prayer A in the *Book of Common Prayer* and Prayer IV in the *Lutheran Book of Worship.* In the petition for the Holy Spirit, according to the original fifth-century Latin text of this prayer, we read:

> And we ask that you would send your holy Spirit upon the offering of your holy church; that, gathering (it) into one, you would grant to all who partake of the holy things (to partake) for the fullness of the holy Spirit for the strengthening *[ad confirmationem]* of faith in truth.[34]

We might say then that what completes baptism, therefore, is the eucharist; what "confirms" baptism, ultimately, is the eucharist. Or to say that another way, the Holy Spirit continuously and repeatedly "confirms" the baptized through their reception of holy communion.

The Feast of Pentecost as a Baptismal Feast

If baptism and the Holy Spirit go together inseparably, then surely the feast of Pentecost readily suggests itself, together with Easter and Epiphany, as another prime occasion for the celebration of baptism within the ongoing life of the church. In fact, according to the New Testament, the *only* biblical festival with which baptisms are intimately associated is not Passover-Easter but *precisely* Pentecost, where in Acts 2:37–42, "three thousand" were baptized in response to Peter's obviously powerful Pentecost proclamation. That's a rather impressive precedent for viewing Pentecost as a baptismal festival and certainly one to which we are invited to pay attention still today. If Pentecost is the feast of the "birth" of the church, as it is often popularly understood and presented, it is interesting to note that this birth is explicitly about the Apostles being baptized with the fire of the Holy

Spirit (see Acts 2:3 and Luke 3:16) and that the very first act of this newly born church, after proclamation of the word, is, precisely, a liturgical-sacramental act in the baptism of three thousand converts, which leads immediately to their meal sharing in communion *(koinonia)* with the teaching and prayer of the Apostles.

As we saw in chapter 1, when the early-third-century North African theologian Tertullian articulated his preference for Easter-Passover baptism he was quick to add: "After that [Passover], Pentecost is a most auspicious period for arranging baptisms, for during it our Lord's resurrection was several times made known among the disciples and the grace of the Holy Spirit first given."[35] If for Tertullian this reference to the "most auspicious period" of Pentecost means the fifty-day Easter season, because the day of Pentecost was not yet on the calendar as the almost separate "feast" of the Holy Spirit,[36] by the time of the *Verona* or *"Leonine" Sacramentary* in the sixth century, the feast of Pentecost on the fiftieth day of Easter had certainly become itself an occasion for celebrating baptism in the Roman church. Within that document, as we saw in the previous chapter, it is precisely in relationship to Pentecost where the liturgical texts for baptism are included and where a special baptismal Mass is provided. Together with Easter, Pentecost remained on the liturgical books of the West as one of the two preferred occasions for baptismal celebration (see both the *Gelasian* and *Gregorian* sacramentaries).

It may well be the case, in terms of the historical development of the feast of Pentecost, that either during the fifty-day Pentecost period or on the day of Pentecost itself, baptism was generally celebrated as a kind of "overflow" from Easter for those unable, for whatever reason, to be baptized at Easter itself, especially since the kind of fasting and ascetical preparation required of candidates for baptism would be incongruent with the rejoicing and celebration associated with the Easter season.[37] But it is also possible that baptism during or on Pentecost actually reflects the liturgical memory of a much earlier baptismal preference in some areas of primitive Christianity, a preference which may predate the almost universal acceptance of the theoretical norm for Easter baptism itself in the late fourth- and early fifth-century church. In his recent doctoral dissertation on the development of the Jerusalem liturgical calendar, for example, Walter Ray has suggested, however tentatively, that the description of Pentecost baptism in Acts 2:37–42 may, in fact, reflect the liturgical practice of the early Jerusalem church, which was only later changed to conform to the developing preference for Easter.[38] Indeed, given the biblical precedent for Pentecost baptism in Acts, it is somewhat ironic that Pentecost baptism would become merely the occasion for the baptismal overflow from Easter.

But whatever the historical situation may have been, certainly in our own day the feast of Pentecost can be recovered as another prime occasion for baptism, even within the context of a full Pentecost vigil at the grand culmination of Easter's fifty days. It would not take much to bring this about. While the celebration of baptism at Pentecost is strongly suggested in the American Episcopal *Book of Common Prayer,* it is odd that no baptismal vigil comparable to the "Vigil for the Eve of the Baptism of Our Lord," which was discussed in the previous chapter, is provided for Pentecost in the *Book of Occasional Services.* This *Book of Occasional Services,* however, does offer "A Vigil on the Eve of Baptism," which is designed to take place on the evening before whenever baptism might be celebrated.[39] If not specifically oriented to Pentecost, some of the suggested vigil readings—Exodus 19:1–9a, 16–20a; 20:18–20 (The Story of the Covenant); Ezekiel 36:24–28 (A New Heart and a New Spirit); Ezekiel 37:1–14 (The Valley of Dry Bones); and Romans 8: 14–17 (We Are Children of God)—are quite obviously appropriate for Pentecost. Similarly, the four optional readings from the Hebrew Bible already assigned to the Pentecost Vigil Mass in the current Roman lectionary—Genesis 11:1–9 (The Tower of Babel); Exodus 19:3–8, 16–20 (The Giving of the Law on Mt. Sinai); Ezekiel 37:1–14 (The Dry Bones and New Life); and Joel 3:1–5 (The Gift of the Spirit)—together with Romans 8: 22–27 as the epistle reading and John 7:37–39 as the gospel would already provide a suitable vigil to which the celebration of baptism could easily be attached, if instead of selecting only one of the Hebrew Bible readings all four options would be read with appropriate responses and concluding prayers.

Such an adaptation for an "extended Pentecost vigil" was already suggested for Roman Catholic liturgical usage in the 1988 Circular Letter of the Vatican Congregation for Divine Worship, *Concerning the Preparation and Celebration of the Easter Feasts,* which unfortunately says that this vigil, unlike the Easter Vigil is one "whose character is not baptismal."[40] And the recently revised sacramentary, which has been approved by the bishops of the United States and is awaiting confirmation from Rome, may well include a nine-reading vigil that parallels the Easter Vigil itself, including, along with the above six readings from the current Roman Pentecost Vigil Mass, Genesis 2:4b–10, 18, 21–25 (Watering of the Earth and Creation), Proverbs 8:22–31 (Witness of the Master Worker; Rejoicing before the Lord); and Jeremiah 31:31–34 (The New Covenant) together with appropriate responses and concluding prayers.

As with the Easter Vigil readings, which already provide a classic typological biblical commentary on the paschal imagery of baptism, so a Pentecost Vigil constituted by these readings provides a similar baptismal commentary on the relationship of baptism and the Holy Spirit. Indeed, contrary to the directive of the Circular Letter *Concerning the Preparation and Celebration of the Easter Feasts,* how could this Pentecost vigil *not* be baptismal in character, just as it was already in the medieval Roman sacramentaries? For Pentecost as the celebration of the gift and breath of the Holy Spirit welling up in believers (John 7), the reversal of the scattering and confusion of the Tower of Babel (Genesis 11), the resurrection of Israel's dry bones by the "wind" of the Spirit (Ezekiel 37), the giving of the Law at Mount Sinai (Exodus 19) and the new covenant in Christ (Jeremiah 31) is nothing other than baptism par excellence. Indeed, as in the case of the three thousand converts added to the church after Peter's Pentecost homily in Acts 2, the only proper response to the great Mystery of Pentecost is "Brothers [and sisters], what should we do?" And the only answer to that is still: "Repent and be baptized every one of you in the name of Jesus Christ so that your sins may be forgiven, and you will receive the gift of the Holy Spirit." Pentecost, without the celebration of baptism, seems, in this light, to be rather incomplete and lacking.

In arguing for the recovery of Pentecost baptism as a way to reappropriate the imagery of the connection between baptism and the Holy Spirit, I am well aware of certain problems, especially with regard to adult initiation and the catechumenate. We are so well organized today with the lenten catechumenate, its scrutiny and other rites and so oriented toward Easter baptism that placing a similar emphasis on Pentecost as anything other than a stopgap or catchall for those who missed Easter baptism might be rather difficult to accomplish. If celebrating the baptism of infants and young children at Pentecost would be relatively easy and, as with the baptismal image of new birth and adoption in water *and the Holy Spirit,* may be highly appropriate in the case of infant baptism, even within the context of a Pentecost vigil, adult initiation at this time brings with it its own set of issues.

At the same time, however, the fifty days of the Easter season are, thanks to Lent and Easter Vigil baptism, *already* marked by attention to baptismal mystagogy in the life of the church, especially for those who are baptized at Easter. But if the Easter season is already mystagogical in character, certainly the Sunday readings for this season, especially (but not only) in Year A of the lectionary, are equally appropriate for prebaptismal catechesis and formation as well.

Where do we find better biblical-liturgical catechesis on faith than the account of "Doubting Thomas" on Easter 2 (John 20:19–31), on the eucharist than in the Emmaus narrative on Easter 3 (Luke 24:13–35), on the Good Shepherd who "seals" us in baptism to give us life than on Easter 4 (John 10:1–10), on our baptismal identity as a "chosen race and royal priesthood" on Easter 5 (1 Peter 2:4–9), on the relationship between baptism and the Holy Spirit and the promise of not being left as orphans on Easter 6 (Acts 8:5–8, 14–17; John 14:15–21), on the connection between baptism and the Holy Spirit and the dominical institution of baptism itself on the feast of the Ascension (Acts 1:1–11; Matthew 28:16–20), or on the corporate and intimate identity of the church with Christ for whom Jesus himself prays in his highly priestly prayer on Easter 7 (John 17:1–11)? Indeed, the Easter season may be interpreted just as oriented catechetically toward baptism on Pentecost as the lenten season is oriented catechetically toward Easter baptism. In other words, both seasons are potentially catechetical and mystagogical at the same time and either season certainly "works" for prebaptismal formation.

If we have tended to interpret these readings mystagogically in light of Easter baptism, the recovery of an equally ancient Pentecost baptismal focus in service to the inseparable connection between baptism and the Holy Spirit might invite us to reread these Easter season texts with catechetical eyes. And, theoretically at least, even prebaptismal scrutiny rites might well be adapted or composed for Sundays 4, 5 and 6 of the Easter season, where the readings are certainly more concerned with the meaning of baptism. If nothing else, the celebration of Pentecost itself urges us to pay attention to its baptismal connotations and, as such, if not baptism itself, certainly rites of baptismal renewal and sprinkling need to be celebrated on Pentecost. Surely the relationship between baptism and the Holy Spirit, which this feast underscores and highlights powerfully, needs to be a central focus in both our baptismal catechesis and mystagogy in service to whenever baptism is celebrated.

Conclusion

The current rites of baptism clearly demonstrate the significance and central role of the Holy Spirit. Both baptism and eucharist may rightly be called "sacraments of the Holy Spirit." While our own Western theological and sacramental tradition has not been all that articulate on the Spirit's presence, activity and role, the current Roman rites of baptism, initially called for by the Second Vatican Council, and the rites of several other churches today are filled with an imaginative and rich baptismal theology of the Spirit. And, because the Holy Spirit can no more be separated from baptism than from the Trinity, we would do well to recover and pay close attention to the role of the Holy Spirit in our baptismal catechesis, celebration and mystagogy today.

Questions about faith, justification, spirituality, ecclesiology, eschatology and the meaning of the eucharist are ultimately always questions about the Holy Spirit and the Spirit's role in forming people as believers in and disciples of Christ. Faith itself is nothing other than the Spirit-given ability to trust and believe in God and to confess Jesus as the living Lord. Our justification, our being set in a right relationship with God and each other, is nothing other than that which is graciously and freely given to us by the working of the Holy Spirit and by which we come to faith. Our spirituality, our ongoing life in Christ, is nothing other than the very Spirit of Easter-Pentecost breathing within us, the fruit of Jesus' own death and resurrection. The church is nothing other than that *koinonia,* fellowship or communion of the Spirit into which baptism brings us. Our eschatological hope for the future has been sealed at baptism by the down payment of the Spirit in our hearts. And the eucharist itself is nothing other than the action and meal by which the Holy Spirit continues to make us what our baptism into the Mystery of Christ has already made us to be, the very body of Christ we receive and celebrate in order to be sent on mission *(Ite, missa est)* as that body in the world.

Several years ago, Frederick Dale Bruner and William Hordern wrote a short book on the theology of the Holy Spirit called *The Holy Spirit—Shy Member of the Trinity.*[41] The title says it all. The Holy Spirit is not pneumato-centric but always christocentric and theocentric, always directed toward Christ and always directing us toward Christ for wholeness, life and salvation. As the Swedish theologian Regin Prenter wrote in his classic study, *Spiritus Creator,* "The Holy Spirit makes the crucified and risen Christ such a present and redeeming reality to us that faith in Christ and conformity to Christ spring directly from this reality."[42] Similarly, according to Prenter, the Holy Spirit is the one who "takes the crucified and risen Christ out of the remoteness of history and heavenly glory and places him as a living and redeeming reality in the midst of our life with its suffering, inner conflict and death."[43] This is *precisely* why, of course, we cannot afford to separate the Holy Spirit from baptism, or from any of the sacramental-liturgical rites of the church and why the recovery of this "shy," often hidden and behind-the-scenes but central role of the Holy Spirit, indeed of the Trinitarian Mystery of God, is so necessary in our catechesis, celebration and ongoing mystagogy in those rites. **103**

I have suggested in this chapter that one way to recover the integral and necessary connection between the Holy Spirit and baptism is to reconsider the feast of Pentecost as a baptismal feast and occasion. While I am aware that such an emphasis may raise all kinds of pastoral and other problems, I believe fully that the key to understanding and, hence, celebrating both the "Fifty Days" and the "Fiftieth Day" itself is primarily baptism, just as it was for the three thousand who responded to Peter's original Pentecost homily in Acts 2:37–42. Without a baptismal foundation in the Holy Spirit, the Spirit of God "who raised Jesus from the dead" and who dwells within us (Romans 8:11), the one Spirit in whom we were baptized and of whom we drink in the eucharist (1 Corinthians 12:13), then Pentecost is not Pentecost. And, like Easter itself, Pentecost is a baptismal feast par excellence because baptism itself is the sacrament and "seal" of the Holy Spirit, and it is this whenever it is celebrated. But just how confirmation as a *separated* sacrament of the seal of the Holy Spirit fits into all of this, if it does, is a another topic for another time.

Chapter 4

Baptism as Incorporation into the Body of Christ

■

> For just as the body is one and has many members and all the members of the body, though many, are one body, so it is with Christ. For in the one Spirit we were all baptized into one body—Jews or Greeks, slaves or free—and we were all made to drink of one Spirit. (1 Corinthians 12:12–13)

> There is one body and one Spirit, just as you were called to the one hope of your calling, one Lord, one faith, one baptism, one God and Father of all, who is above all and through all and in all. (Ephesians 4:4–6)

> But you are a chosen race, a royal priesthood, a holy nation, God's own people, in order that you may proclaim the mighty acts of him who called you out of darkness into his marvelous light. Once you were not a people, but now you are God's people; once you had not received mercy, but now you have received mercy. (1 Peter 2:9–10)

Whatever image or model of baptism might be our primary or dominant one—whether baptism as participation in the death, burial and resurrection of Christ, baptism as new birth and/or adoption through water and the Holy Spirit, or baptism as the seal of the Holy Spirit—baptism is also and always about our initiation, our incorporation into that people of God called church, the body of Christ. So common is this understanding that we even refer to baptism, confirmation and first communion themselves as the rites or sacraments of **105**

Christian *initiation*. But initiation or incorporation into what? Well, initiation and incorporation into Christ by the power and gift of the Holy Spirit, of course, but because Christ himself cannot be separated from his body the church, incorporation also into his body at the same time. It is not that we are first initiated into union and communion with Christ and *then* as a consequence into the community of the church. Rather, baptism itself signifies and effects both at the same time. It can do nothing other than this. The church into which we are baptized is the same church that, in obedience to the command of Christ (Matthew 28:19), actually baptizes, and so, through this baptismal action and event, incorporates new members of Christ into itself. Hence, communion with Christ means communion with the church, and communion with the church means, simultaneously, communion with Christ. To separate faith in Christ from active membership and participation in his body can be done only at great peril. Faith in Christ implies faith that the church is his body. Even the Nicene Creed, which we regularly confess in our liturgical assemblies, makes belief "*in* the one, holy, catholic and apostolic church" part of our common and ecumenical profession of baptismal faith.

One of the great insights in modern Roman Catholic ecclesiology has been precisely the recovery of the sacramental nature of the church and its identity in the world as the great sacrament of salvation.[1] Long associated with Dominican theologian Edward Schillebeeckx[2] and Jesuit theologian Karl Rahner,[3] this sacramental understanding of the church's identity means that just as the Incarnate Christ himself through his word and act was (and is) the primordial or *Ur* sacrament of God's saving encounter with the world, so too is the church, primarily in its proclamation and sacramental-liturgical activity, the continuation of that saving and grace-filled encounter with God in history. Consequently, both the church and the sacraments themselves are but the human and embodied extension of Christ's own incarnation in space, time and history. It is through this community of grace and through its actions that Christ continues to encounter us in saving grace and that we simultaneously encounter Christ in his abiding real presence. Yes, Christ himself baptizes, but Christ does so only through and by means of his body the church. Yes, the church itself ritualizes, celebrates and prays for God to act in its sacramental rites, but the prayer it voices "through Christ our Lord" is also, simultaneously, the living and effective prayer of Christ himself in us and for us! For a Roman Catholic today, then, the question of how many sacraments there are in the church must always receive the answer of at least "nine": Christ himself, the church and those seven distinct "sacraments" by which and in which the church expresses its identity and so comes to be itself.

If such an understanding has been an obvious characteristic approach in modern Roman Catholic ecclesiology, it has by no means been entirely absent from Protestantism, especially Lutheranism, even if ecclesiology itself has not been a hallmark of Protestant theology in general. Dietrich Bonhoeffer was one Protestant ecclesiologist who certainly approached such a sacramental understanding of the church. In *Christ the Center* he wrote:

> Just as Christ is present as the Word and in the Word, as the sacrament and in the sacrament, so too he is also present as community and in the community. . . . Christ is the community by virtue of his being *pro me*. His form, indeed his only form, is the community between the ascension and the second coming. . . . What does it mean that Christ . . . is also community? It means that the Logos of God has extension in space and time in and as the community. . . . [T]he Word is also itself community insofar as the community is itself revelation and the Word wills to have the form of a created body....The community is the body of Christ. Body here is not just a metaphor. The community is the body of Christ, it does not *represent* the body of Christ. Applied to the community, the

> concept of the body is not just a functional concept which merely refers to the members of this body; it is a comprehensive and central concept of the mode of existence of the one who is present in his exaltation and his humiliation.[4]

More recently, contemporary Lutheran theologian Carl Braaten also has sought to restore for Protestants a sacramental understanding of the church, writing specifically of the eucharist in this context: "What defines the church is the living presence incarnate in the eucharist, where Christ and his community are bodily one. *The church is Christ as his bodily presence in the world,* prefiguring the future of the world in the kingdom of God."[5]

To be initiated or incorporated into Christ by baptism, therefore, means to be initiated or incorporated into the church, just as being initiated or incorporated into the church also means being initiated or incorporated into Christ. If we have our "church as body of Christ" ecclesiology correct, then saying only one of these (e.g., baptism is initiation into the church) already naturally and necessarily implies the other (i.e., baptism is initiation into Christ).

The Community into Which the Baptized Are Incorporated

Having our ecclesiology correct today, however, is not always an easy thing to do. Such a high sacramental ecclesiology, as summarized above, can sometimes run the risk of becoming what we might call "ecclesiolatry," that is, a turning of the church into an idol, either by equating *every* act and pronouncement of the church as being that of Christ himself or by so closely identifying the relationship of Christ and the church that the distinction between head and members is blurred. But an equal danger results when this close and essential relationship between Christ and the church is ignored and not at the forefront of our theological-ecclesiological consciousness.

In his critique of the model of the church as "people of God" or "community," Avery Dulles correctly reminded us years ago that the church is much more than a human association or community of like-minded individuals:

> While the church promises communion, it does not always provide it in very evident form. Christians commonly experience the church more as a companionship of fellow travelers on the same journey than as a union of lovers dwelling in the same home. Gregory Baum expresses some wise reservations about the tendency of some . . . to drift into underground churches in the hope of finding some more ideal type of community: "Some people involved in the underground are eagerly looking for the perfect human community. They long for a community which fulfills all their needs and in terms of which they are able to define themselves. This search is illusory, especially in our own day when to be human means to participate in several communities and to remain critical in regard to all of them. The longing desire for the warm and understanding total community is the search for the good mother, which is bound to end in disappointment and heartbreak. There are no good mothers and fathers, there is only the divine mystery summoning and freeing us to grow up."[5]

When a proper ecclesiological understanding of the church as the body of Christ, not in its metaphorical or representational sense but in its real sense is neglected or ignored, the great danger is that other romantic notions of the church as an idealized human "family" or "community" can so easily take its place. We end up either settling for something less than this ecclesiology actually means or, when such expectations are not realized, the church itself becomes rejected by those seeking to "belong" in order to have their perceived psychic, social and relational "needs" met. In other words, we may think we know what community is, and so we put all kinds of unrealistic warm, gushy, expectations of closeness and intimacy into our understanding and end up being frustrated when such things don't materialize. We think sometimes that "real" Christian community should provide the intimacy of a small group of like-minded people who share the same experiences and values, a family, a living room gathering or a mountain-top retreat experience. Think here of the common ideological rhetoric in our day and age about parishes as families that we are invited to join or to which we are invited to belong. Think also of the kinds of intimate experiences of community formed in and by small-group sharing so common in the catechumenal process today. But to expect that such experiences, real though they surely are, should be part and parcel of Christian community is not wise! "We forget," writes James Dallen,

> that an old tradition sees the feeding of the *multitudes* as the institution of the eucharist . . . ; that the major parable Jesus told about community [the Good Samaritan] concerned the relationship of two *strangers*. We forget the Emmaus story, where two disciples find the Risen Christ not in their friendship but when they reach out to a stranger. [emphasis added]

He continues:

> Look again at the parable of the Good Samaritan—that's what it means to be neighbor, that's what it means to be community. That goes against the grain of our society. Our society, our culture, conditions and forms us to look out for number one. Thus liturgy that builds toward social justice is liturgy that moves us out of our cultural individualism into a realization of communion, common union. It does so by enabling us to interact in ways that contest and counter the commonsense structures and stereotypes of our culture where we compete to get ahead, we look out for ourselves and our own. It then challenges us to transform those structures and stereotypes into realizations of the reign of God where there is really liberty and justice for all, where we strive not to be number one but to be one.[7]

As hinted at already, especially problematic in our contemporary cultural pursuit of community, closeness and intimacy, conceived of in rather romantic and/or idealized manners, is the way in which the church as body of Christ is often co-opted in support of various "community-building" ideologies or methods. The result is the liturgical celebration of homogenous and shared values that becomes the means for forming such community. Franciscan author Kenneth Himes notes that if the church

> is to say something to our culture, then the church must bring people together in ways that go beyond the ordinary patterns of association in our society. The poor and the rich, the old and the young, black and white, weak and powerful—our nation experiences polarization in so many areas. If liturgical congregations mirror such division, then the witness value of . . . community is muted. . . . Some newer forms of liturgical community run the risk of becoming gatherings of like-minded persons who are "comfortable" with each other. . . . [But] there is a risk of establishing forms of worship that merely reinforce what Robert Bellah has called "lifestyle enclaves," . . . [that is,] "ways of being together with our own kind." . . . [But] liturgy as the celebration of a faith community presupposes participants who are willing to "reach across the social, political and economic barriers that structure our world to say 'Our Father' and to speak of themselves as 'we.' "[8]

Similarly, Nathan Mitchell writes of this approach:

> Neither the church nor its liturgy aims at forming an intimate, homogenous fellowship of familiars united by the same socioeconomic status and espousing identical middle-class values. On the contrary, in the earliest decades of its existence the Christian movement (as represented especially by its maverick missionary Paul) consciously chose pluralism over parochialism. This meant that the churches would be multicultural, multi-ethnic, multiracial—places where a stranger could share a meal with strangers (just as Jesus has done in his ministry). It meant that Christian unity would result not from ideological conformity but from welcoming "conflict as an opportunity to learn that our wholeness lies in the One who sustains us all." It meant that Christian identity would result not from the suppression of diversity or difference but from the recognition that free people can form communities "where difference does not lead to judgment, where diversity does not breed distrust." . . . [C]ommunity arises not from the ideology of intimacy, nor from the rejection of public life, nor from middle-class values of "joining" and "participation in approved groups," but from the company of strangers, from the recognition that we are all "outside the camp," that "we

111

have here no lasting city," that we are all "aliens, pilgrims and sojourners" (see Hebrews 11:13; 13:13–14; 1 Peter 2:11).[9]

A proper understanding of the church as body of Christ does not permit us to romanticize concepts like "family" and "community" when speaking of its corporate-communal identity. The church *is* both "family" and "community," and baptism itself certainly constitutes a brand-new network of divine and human family relationships in which strangers become brothers and sisters and in which, by the gift of the Holy Spirit, we are enabled corporately and individually to address God intimately as our "Abba" in prayer (see Galatians 4:6). But ecclesiologically, concepts like "family" and "community" transcend our own limited notions and experience of what these mean, and the analogy is, at best, only partially true.

The issue is not one of closeness and intimacy. The issue is not homogeneity where everyone thinks alike, talks alike and, essentially, looks alike. The issue is whether or not the community formed by baptism and continually re-formed by the eucharist is a place of hospitality to strangers, where people can come to realize their coming-into-union with each other in Christ, in spite of and rejoicing in, their differences; where people can find a supportive context in which to disagree in love over potentially divisive issues; a place where *people* united *in Christ* rather than ideologies or agendas are the principal focus. Only a community that finds its center in having been made the body of Christ himself in baptism and in receiving the body of Christ given and blood of Christ shed for it in the eucharist so that it may be that body for others *(Ite, missa est!)* can be that kind of community in the world. The real issue is this: "In the sacraments, the gospel made visible, we experience the reign of God and go out as the Body of Christ to make it a reality for all. The Body of Christ, that's the key! If we can believe that, we can believe anything. If we can believe that, we can change the world."[10]

The church as the body of Christ *is* the key. Again, it is Dietrich Bonhoeffer's clear reflection on the nature of Christian community that can assist us in coming to terms with what our baptismal incorporation into this body both means and does *not* mean. In his classic theological meditation on Christian community, *Life Together,* Bonhoeffer dealt specifically with the occasional conflict between human expectations of "community" and the gift of authentic Christian community itself:

> Christian community has not been given to us by God for us to be constantly taking its temperature. . . . Christian brotherhood is not an ideal which we must realize; it is rather a reality created by God in Christ in which we may participate. The more clearly we learn to recognize that the ground and strength and promise of all our fellowship is in Jesus Christ alone, the more serenely shall we think of our fellowship and pray and hope for it.[11]

Elsewhere in the same study he adds:

> There is probably no Christian to whom God has not given the uplifting experience of genuine Christian community at least once in his life. But in this world such experiences can be no more than a gracious extra beyond the daily bread of Christian community life. We have no claim upon such experiences and we do not live with other Christians for the sake of acquiring them. It is not the experience of Christian brotherhood, but solid and certain faith in brotherhood that holds us together. That God has acted and wants to act upon us all, this we see in faith as God's greatest gift, this makes us glad and happy, but it also makes us ready to forego all such experiences when God at times does not grant them. We are bound together by faith, not by experience.[12]

Baptism, therefore, is not initiation or incorporation into "community," vaguely or romantically understood, but it is initiation into a particular *kind* of community, which may or may not offer that sense or "experience" of intimacy, joining or belonging that many seek. For this community, which understands itself to be nothing less than the corporate Christ himself, Christ existing *as* church in the world between his ascension and coming again, is a community sent on mission in that world to proclaim and mediate in its sacramental being the profound grace-filled invitation to enter into the ultimate eschatological community we call the "reign" or "kingdom of God." Such a community is, simultaneously, a royal community of priests in the one Priest Jesus Christ, an ecumenical and inclusive catholic community in the one Christ, who is not divided, and a community that knows itself to be a "communion of saints" in Christ. Each of these dimensions of the body of Christ calls for additional comment.

Church as a Priestly Community

In chapter 1, I suggested that interpreting baptism as our participation in the death, burial and resurrection of Christ might best suggest a baptismal ecclesiology of servanthood, that is, a model of the church as servant that seeks to embrace the cross in its mission of solidarity and service in the world in continuity with Christ's own mission. Such a servant model is, precisely, a priestly model at the same time as this community of priests, constituted by baptism, offers itself in union with Christ *the* Priest for the life of the world. Probably nothing in the contemporary rites of baptism better expresses this understanding than the postbaptismal anointing in the current Roman Rite, an anointing that, unfortunately, is customarily omitted in favor of confirmation in the case of adult initiation:

> The God of power and Father of our Lord Jesus Christ
> has freed you from sin
> and brought you to new life
> through water and the Holy Spirit.
> He now anoints you with the chrism of salvation
> so that, united with his people,
> you may remain forever a member of Christ,
> who is Priest, Prophet and King.[13]

A similar understanding of this priestly identity of the church appears also in the words that introduce the welcoming spoken to the newly baptized by the assembly at the conclusion of the baptismal rite in *Lutheran Book of Worship:* "Through baptism God has made *these* new *sisters and brothers members* of the priesthood we all share in Christ Jesus, that we may proclaim the praise of God and bear his creative and redeeming Word to all the world."[14]

Because it is the body of *Christ* into which the baptized are incorporated, all are initiated by baptism into a royal and prophetic priesthood. As such, the community of the church is a particular kind of community, one that knows itself as engaged in active priestly ministry and self-sacrificial service in the world. The body of Christ is not a community bent on its own survival or self-preservation. The body of Christ, who is Priest, Prophet and King, exists that it may die in Christ, so that it may extend itself for the life of others as it continues its baptismal pilgrimage through death to resurrection. The current *Catechism of the Catholic Church* expresses this baptismal-ecclesiological dimension well:

> The baptized have become "living stones" to be "built into a spiritual house, to be a holy priesthood." By baptism they share in the priesthood of Christ, in his prophetic and royal mission. They are "a chosen race, a royal priesthood, a holy nation, God's own people, that [they] may declare the wonderful deeds of him who called [them] out of darkness into his marvelous light." *Baptism gives a share in the common priesthood of all believers.*[15]

In other words, baptism itself is an "ordination" to priesthood, and the church itself is nothing other than a royal, prophetic and communal priesthood itself. In an article devoted in large part to precisely this priestly identity of the baptized, Aidan Kavanagh writes:

> A baptismal element needs to be introduced into our contemporary discussion of ministry. . . . But while one cannot discuss baptism without ministerial implications arising, it has

unfortunately become usual to discuss ministries without ever feeling it necessary to enter into the implications of this discussion for baptism. That holy orders are rooted in baptism never seems to cross our minds. I suggest that it must. . . . [T]he church baptizes to priesthood: it ordains only to executive exercise of that priesthood in the major orders of ministry. Indeed *Ordo Romanus XI* of the ninth century has the baptized and anointed neophytes vested in stole and chasuble as they are presented to the Bishop of Rome for consignation prior to the beginning of the Easter eucharist. The point being that *sacerdotium* (priesthood) in orthodox Christianity is not plural but single. It is that of Christ, shared among those in solidarity with whom . . . he was himself baptized in the Jordan and also in solidarity with whom he now stands as both sacrifice and sacrificer in heaven. . . . While every presbyter and bishop is therefore a sacerdotal person, not every sacerdotal person in the church is a presbyter or bishop. Nor does sacerdotality come upon one for the first time, so to speak, at one's ordination. In constant genesis in the font, the church is born there as a sacerdotal assembly by the Spirit of the Anointed One himself. *Laos* ["laity"] is a priestly name for a priestly person.[16]

He continues:

. . . [I]n baptism by water and the Holy Spirit . . . one is anointed with as full a sacerdotality as the church possesses in and by the Anointed One himself. Ordination cannot make one more priestly than the church, and without baptism ordination cannot make one a priest at all. Becoming a Christian and becoming a sacerdotal being are not merely correlative processes, they are one and the same.[17]

To be baptized, therefore, to be incorporated by baptism into the body of Christ, is to become a priest within a community of priests in Jesus Christ, our great High Priest. However the specific ministries of bishop, presbyter and deacon are ordered in the life of the church, all the baptized, children, men and women alike, share in this common priesthood of service and offering in union with Christ himself and all theological reflection on the priesthood of Christ and the church must begin here at the font. Yes, because of baptism, the Roman Catholic

Church has several women *priests,* although it does not have women bishops, presbyters and deacons.

The Community of the Church as an Ecumenical-Inclusive-Catholic Community

In chapter 1, I drew attention to the fact that a "dead church," which knows itself to be dead and buried by baptism into Christ, can afford to risk itself ecumenically in the pursuit of full and visible Christian unity because it knows already that common Christian identity it shares, having been brought to "newness of life" out of a common watery grave. Again, it is the 1982 Faith and Order statement of the World Council of churches, *Baptism, Eucharist, Ministry,* that underscores this ecumenical foundation of baptism well:

> Administered in obedience to our Lord, baptism is a sign and seal of our common discipleship. Through baptism, Christians are brought into union with Christ, with each other and with the church of every time and place. Our common baptism, which unites us to Christ in faith, is thus a basic bond of unity. We are one people, and all are called to confess and serve one Lord in each place and in the entire world. The union with Christ which we share through baptism has important implications for Christian unity. "There is . . . one baptism, one God and Father of us all . . . " (Ephesians 4:4–6). When baptismal unity is realized in one, holy, catholic, apostolic church, a genuine Christian witness can be made to the healing and reconciling love of God. Therefore, our one baptism into Christ constitutes a call to the churches to overcome their divisions and visibly manifest their fellowship.[18]

The *Catechism of the Catholic Church* similarly highlights the ecumenical nature of the church due to baptism, while acknowledging the tragic divisions that continue to exist:

> Baptism constitutes the foundation of communion among all Christians, including those who are not yet in full communion with the Catholic church: "For men who believe in Christ and

have been properly baptized are put in some, though imperfect, communion with the Catholic church. Justified by faith in baptism, [they] are incorporated into Christ; they therefore have a right to be called Christians and with good reason are accepted as brothers by the children of the Catholic Church." Baptism therefore constitutes *the sacramental bond of unity* existing among all who through it are reborn.[19]

Because the church into which the baptized are incorporated is *already* an ecumenical church, inseparably united by baptism as the *one* body of the *one* Christ, who is not divided (see 1 Corinthians 1:13), Christian unity is, above all, not a demand, not a call, but already a gift to be received and further realized gratefully. The language of the New Testament is clear: "There is one body and one Spirit, just as you were called to the one hope of your calling, one Lord, one faith, one baptism, one God and Father of all, who is above all and through all and in all" (Ephesians 4:4–6). Through baptism *all* are incorporated into the *one* Christ, the *one* church, the *one* body of Christ. Although we are always baptized within particular ecclesial communities, according to the liturgical rites of those communities and although we live out our baptism in those distinct ecclesial manners of life, we are not really baptized "Catholic," "Lutheran" or anything else. We should strive to remove such an incomplete theology of baptismal identity from our vocabulary. We are baptized into communion with *Christ* and so, into communion with the *one church* of Jesus Christ; i.e., all the baptized, in a very real way, *already* belong to the same church! It is what the documents of Vatican II and the *Catechism of the Catholic Church* call this "sacramental bond of unity" that must be on the forefront of any discussion of visible Christian unity today.

Any catechesis on baptism, therefore, that fails to take into account the ecumenical nature of baptism and the church is not only incomplete and partial baptismal catechesis but incomplete ecclesiology as well. If the ecumenical goal is to realize this baptismal "communion among all Christians" more perfectly in a full and visible communion of the churches, the most important step toward that goal is the realization of this communion that already exists sacramentally between us. If *Christ himself* is not divided, then how dare we be? Indeed, the division of the church is nothing other than a shameful and sinful scandal, which casts into doubt not only the credibility of the church's identity and mission in the world ("a house divided against itself cannot stand," see Mark 3:25), but the claims we want to make about the meaning of baptism as well. The document *Baptism, Eucharist, Ministry* is correct in asserting, "Our one baptism into Christ constitutes a call to the churches to overcome their divisions and visibly manifest their fellowship." If the second millennium of our common ecclesial history in both East and West can be characterized as being marked by the scandal of Christian division, then, perhaps, by the will and grace of God, this third Christian millennium can be the time in which Christian unity is finally restored. But it won't happen without attention to what our one baptism has already made us to be, that is, *Christ* existing as church in the world!

If the body of Christ into which the baptized are incorporated is already *one* body in the *one* Christ, however, then it is also constituted by baptism itself as an inclusive or, more precisely, a "catholic" body, which transcends all categories of race, ethnicity, social-economic status and gender. I have written of the implications of this elsewhere, saying in part that

> we dare not forget that by baptism in the church we are quite literally plunged already into a multicultural ecclesial reality in which all the baptized [may] recognize one another in Christ as common brothers and sisters by that watery sacramental bond, which, in this case, at least, is "thicker than blood." . . . Multiculturalism is not merely a social challenge or issue to be addressed in our rapidly changing and shrinking world . . . Rather, because of the place of baptism multiculturalism **119**

already is a given in the church, a reality and a gift to be cherished, a place where all . . . are welcomed by a common bath
into a common home. The challenge before us . . . is to allow
this baptismal reality to develop and grow in our ecclesial
consciousness that we may become more fully what and who
our baptism has made us to be already, a richly diverse people
of God, the body of Christ, indeed Christ Himself existing as
community in the world. . . . [20]

Nathan Mitchell also underscores this radically inclusive nature of the church constituted by baptism:

We need to redefine church not as "family" but as "halfway
house, moving people from fear of the world around them
into a role as cocreators of a world which is both God's and
their own." . . . This can best be done by reaffirming Paul's
bold, pluralistic blueprint for *inclusive* churches where "there is
neither Jew nor Greek, slave nor free, male nor female, for all
are one in Christ Jesus." Genuine pluralism does not need—
or try—to homogenize experience, tame traditions, exclude
innovation or devalue diversity. It begins, instead, with the
recognition that no single tradition (be it biblical, Western,
American or whatnot) possesses all the resources needed to deal
with the bewildering challenges of modern public life. Rich
as these traditions are, notes Robert Bellah, "if we cling obsti-
nately to them alone we will be guilty of a narrow and . . .
ultimately self-destructive parochialism. We must be able to
embrace the experience of the rootedness of the American
Indians, the uprootedness of the Blacks, the emptiness of the
Asians, not out of some charitable benevolence but because
our own traditions are simply not enough. Cultural defen-
siveness will be fatal. *If we are to survive on this earth, we must
embrace the entire human tradition, make all of it . . . available to
our imagination.*"[21]

Like the gift of Christian unity flowing from baptism,
this radically inclusive or catholic vision of the body of
Christ as a community of equals is not simply a goal but
a reality. Yet, like the continual challenge of Christian
unity, it is, at the same time, a reality to be increasingly
realized in the life of the church. We do not yet know
what a church that takes seriously its multicultural and
120　gender-neutral baptismal plunge into Christ will look

like in the coming years. The contributions of Hispanics, Asians, African Americans, women and other groups to the church in the United States will profoundly affect its identity and mission. What will it mean when the Roman Catholic Church in the United States, for example, is over 50 percent Latino-Hispanic? What will such changes mean for liturgical inculturation and adaptation? What will years of pastoral leadership of women, even if not ordained to the ministries of episcopate, presbyterate and diaconate in the Roman Catholic Church, come to mean ultimately for the ways in which local parishes are organized for ministry, for how pastoral care is provided, for how liturgy is celebrated, for how theology is actually done and taught and for how God comes to be imaged? We cannot say.

And yet, what is at stake in all of this is the very question of "catholicity" itself, of what it means to embrace a baptismal vision of catholic wholeness in Christ. And, like ecumenism itself, that vision and reality are already baptismal gifts to be cherished and realized. Hence, any baptismal catechesis or ecclesiology that dares to ignore this baptismal vision and reality is, at best, incomplete and partial catechesis. For the body of Christ into which one is incorporated is already this kind of community by definition because Christ himself transcends all divisions.

The Community of the Church as the "Communion of Saints"

The body of Christ into which the baptized are incorporated is not only an ecumenical community nor only a community that transcends all other ethnic, racial, socioeconomic and gender distinctions. It is, at the same time, a body which, like Christ himself, actually transcends both space and time in a communion that even death **121** itself cannot break apart. In both a broad (all the baptized themselves; see Romans 1:7) and narrow sense (official saints, those who have gone on before us), this body is also rightly identified as the "Communion of Saints." Whether by that designation one means this community as formed by a common *"communio in sacris"* (communion in "holy things") or the community as the *"communio sanctorum"* itself matters little since in either case the designation of "Communion of Saints" is ultimately about the identity of the church in Christ constituted by baptism. To use traditional language, both the "Church Triumphant" and the "Church Militant" are united together in this one Communion of Saints.

One of the most powerful ways that baptism as incorporation into this Communion of Saints is signified liturgically, of course, is by the singing of the Litany of the Saints immediately before the rites of Christian initiation are themselves celebrated at the Easter Vigil in the Roman Rite and, in a shortened form, as part of the Roman Catholic *Rite of Baptism for Children* as well. Such a liturgical act has profound baptismal-ecclesiological implications. For the church into which one is initiated by baptism is a church rooted in history as the locus of God's saving activity throughout the ages and a church in continuity and community in that great "cloud of witnesses" (see Hebrews 11–12) who have been part of that history and are still "living" members of the body. As the Roman Catholic response within the eighth United States Lutheran-Catholic dialogue, *The One Mediator, the Saints and Mary,* says clearly:

> . . . Jesus Christ alone is never merely alone. He is always found in the company of a whole range of his friends, both living and dead. It is a basic Catholic experience that when recognized and appealed to within a rightly ordered faith, these friends of Jesus Christ strengthen one's own sense of communion with Christ. It's all in a family, we might say; we are part of a people. Saints show us how the grace of God may work in a life; they give us bright patterns of holiness; they

pray for us. Keeping company with the saints in the Spirit of Christ encourages our faith. It is simply part of what it means to be Catholic, bonded with millions of other people not only throughout the world, but also through time. Those who have gone on before us in faith are still living members of the body of Christ and in some unimaginable way we are all connected. Within a rightly ordered faith, both liturgical and private honoring of all the saints, of one saint or of St. Mary serves to keep our feet on the gospel path.[22]

Since the question of saints, however, has been and continues to be for some a problematic issue ecumenically, it may appear that I am contradicting what I said about the ecumenical nature of the church constituted by baptism. To the contrary. One of the more interesting developments in contemporary Protestant worship books has been the recovery of rather full sanctoral cycles in their liturgical calendars.[23] The calendar of "Lesser Festivals and Commemorations" in the *Lutheran Book of Worship,* for example, includes not only biblical and apostolic saints together with appointed opening prayers and specific lectionary readings under the category of "Lesser Festivals" but also a rather complete list of saints or witnesses from every age and walk of life under the heading of "Commemorations."[24] Including, with great ecumenical significance, even Pope John XXIII on June 3, together with a type of "Commons" providing opening prayers and lectionary readings for saints, martyrs, missionaries, renewers of the church, renewers of society, pastors and bishops, theologians and artists and scientists,[25] the *Lutheran Book of Worship* offers a rather complete sanctoral cycle. A similar calendar and "Commons" are included also in the American Episcopal *Book of Common Prayer,* though it is not nearly as full as that in the *Lutheran Book of Worship.* Consequently, with this rediscovery of the saints within various Protestant traditions today, very few, I suspect, would find anything to disagree with in the Roman Catholic statement that part of what it means to be a member of the church includes being "bonded with millions of other people not only throughout the world, but also through time. Those who have gone on before us in faith are still living members of the body of Christ and in some unimaginable way we are all connected." Indeed, even the eucharistic preface for the festival of All Saints in the *Lutheran Book of Worship* underscores that within this communion: "in the blessedness of [the] saints [God has] given us a glorious pledge of the hope of our calling; that, *moved by their witness and supported by their fellowship,* we may run with perseverance the race that is set before us and with them receive the unfading crown of glory."[26]

If neither canonization of saints nor explicit invocation of the saints in liturgical or private prayer is a characteristic of Protestantism, this does not mean that either the Communion of Saints or the saints themselves are unimportant. In fact, in the recent Lutheran adaptation of the catechumenal process, *Welcome to Christ,*[27] a version of the Litany of the Saints is actually provided for use at the Easter Vigil. If this Lutheran version is, understandably, more of a litany of "thanksgiving" *for* the saints (e.g., "For Mary, mother of our Lord: Thanks be to God") rather than a direct invocation *of* various saints themselves (e.g., "Holy Mary, Mother of God: Pray for us"), the fact remains that within the context of baptism itself the presence of the Communion of Saints into which the baptized are incorporated, including several figures from the Hebrew Bible (e.g., Sarah and Abraham, Isaac and Rebekah), is certainly noted and highlighted. Indeed, one might surely expect that this Litany of the Saints will somehow find its way into other Lutheran sanctoral festivals and commemorations (e.g., as an entrance hymn for the festival of All Saints?). A similar baptismal remembering of and thanksgiving for the saints in Lutheran worship also appears in the final petition of the suggested intercessions within the baptismal rite:

> We give thanks for all who have gone before us in the faith
> [St. John the Baptist, Mary, the mother of our Lord, apostles
> and martyrs, evangelists and teachers and all those] who by their
> lives have testified to the love of God, especially __name__.
> Lord, in your mercy, Hear our prayer.[28]

And, at least the Lutheran confessional documents acknowledge that "blessed Mary," the "angels," and "the saints in heaven pray for the church in general, as they prayed for the church universal while they were on earth,"[29] even if explicit invocation of them was strongly denied in the overall polemical context of sixteenth-century Europe.

In spite of the potentially divisive issue of "invocation," then, attention to the Communion of Saints is by no means a contradiction to the ecumenical nature of baptism, and, again, baptismal catechesis that fails to do justice to this communion is both incomplete baptismal catechesis and incomplete ecclesiology. The body of Christ is the Communion of Saints. To be incorporated into that body *is* to be incorporated into communion with the "great cloud of witnesses" who have gone on before us and who, according to the Letter to the Hebrews (11–12), fill the great stadium to cheer us on as we follow Christ, our great pioneer in the pilgrimage to the eschatological City of God. In spite of legitimate (though no longer church-dividing) differences in articulating the precise implications of this Communion of Saints, certainly all the baptized can sing the following stanza of the great nineteenth-century hymn, "The Church's One Foundation," with *one* voice:

> Yet she on earth has union
> With God the Three in One,
> And mystic sweet communion
> With those whose rest is won.
> O blessed heavenly chorus!
> Lord, save us by your grace,
> That we, like saints before us
> May see you face to face.[30]

For into that "blessed heavenly chorus" we, who are both already saints and yet called to become the saints we are, have been incorporated by baptism.

The Feast of All Saints as a Baptismal Feast of Ecclesial Identity

Although baptism as incorporation into the body of Christ is always an extremely important part of the meaning and imagery of baptism whenever the rite itself is celebrated, the feast of All Saints on November 1, often transferred to the Sunday following November 1 within various Protestant traditions, suggests itself as a baptismal festival of ecclesial identity and incorporation par excellence. Even the opening prayer for the eucharistic liturgy for this feast in the American Episcopal *Book of Common Prayer* is replete with suggestive baptismal-ecclesiological images:

> Almighty God, *you have knit together your elect in one communion and fellowship in the mystical body of your Son Christ our Lord:* Give us grace so to follow your blessed saints in all virtuous and godly living, that we may come to those ineffable joys that you have prepared for those who truly love you; through Jesus Christ our Lord, who with you and the Holy Spirit lives and reigns, one God, in glory everlasting. *Amen.*[31]

While it might be relatively easy for all Christian traditions to make the feast of All Saints a most solemn public occasion during Ordinary Time for the celebration of baptism, it is, again, the Episcopal Church in the United States that has actually provided us with a model for even a baptismal *vigil* on this feast.[32] In a manner similar to the Easter Vigil itself, following the service of light, or *lucernarium,* from Evening Prayer and the opening prayer quoted above, this "Vigil for the Eve of All Saints' Day or the Sunday After All Saints' Day" continues with at least three of the following suggested readings, together with their appointed psalms or canticles:

Genesis 12:1–18 (The Call of Abraham)

Daniel 6: (1–15) 16–23 (Daniel Delivered from the Lions' Den)

1 Maccabees 2:49–64 (The Testament and Death of Mattathias)

2 Maccabees 6:1–2; 7:1–23 (The Martyrdom of the Seven Brothers)

Ecclesiasticus 44:1–10, 13–14 (The Eulogy of the Ancestors)

Hebrews 11:32 (33–38) 39–12:2 (Surrounded by a Great Cloud of Witnesses)

Revelation 7:2–4, 9–17 (The Reward of the Saints)

Following the reading of the gospel (either Matthew 5:1–12; Matthew 11:27–30; or Matthew 28:1–10, 16–20), this liturgy continues with the sermon or homily, baptism, confirmation and/or a renewal of baptismal vows and culminates in the celebration of the eucharist.

If incorporating such an All Saints' baptismal vigil into our regular liturgical life may be more easily accomplished on a Saturday night when the feast itself is transferred to the Sunday following November 1, especially given the fact that such an event on a weekday in November would usually be most difficult to sustain within our contemporary cultural context, this Episcopal model is well worth pursuing further. For what could be a more appropriate way to underscore baptism as initiation and/or incorporation into the body of Christ, this priestly, ecumenical, inclusive-catholic Communion of Saints, than to celebrate baptism precisely on that occasion when the very nature and identity of the body of Christ, past and present, is such a central focus within our liturgical celebration already? Certainly the Litany of the Saints could be incorporated easily into this, just as it has always been at the celebration of Christian initiation within the Easter Vigil. And the increasingly common Roman Catholic custom of integrating various local relics of the saints and their reliquaries, often with vigil lights burning in front of them, within the liturgical space for this feast could easily be given a profound baptismal interpretation as highlighting the very presence of the Communion of Saints itself, that living "cloud of witnesses" still inseparably bonded to us and into which the newly baptized are now being incorporated.

With careful planning and a little bit of imagination, the feast of All Saints could easily become—like Easter, Pentecost and the feast of the Baptism of our Lord— one of our prime occasions for the celebration of baptism during the liturgical year or even as an occasion for all of the rites of Christian initiation in their fullness. At the very least, the kind of vigil provided in the liturgical books of the Episcopal Church in the United States, suggests for all of us a rich diet of imagery for our ongoing baptismal catechesis and mystagogy on the nature and identity of the church into which the baptized are initiated.

Other feasts in the sanctoral cycle suggest themselves as suitable occasions for baptism as well. Certainly the patronal feast of an individual parish, when the specific identity, history and mission of this particular incarnation of the body of Christ are often highlighted, would be a most suitable time for incorporating new members through baptism into its ongoing life and mission. Indeed, where else is that identity, history and mission properly located if it doesn't somehow flow from baptism?

Certain Marian feasts on the Roman Catholic calendar also have profound baptismal-ecclesiological meaning and significance. Given our long Western Augustinian history of interpreting baptism as liberation from original sin, the December 8 solemnity of the Immaculate Conception of Mary provides not only another possible occasion for baptism but also for baptismal catechesis and mystagogy. That is, in the womb of baptism the church itself has been "conceived immaculately" by water and the Holy Spirit and, if mariology is best understood in relationship to ecclesiology, christology and pneumatology, then there is indeed a close parallel between what is asserted of Mary's conception in service to her ultimate role as the Theotokos ("God-bearer") in the Incarnation and the ultimate role of the church, the community of the baptized, as the God-bearers of the Incarnate Christ in the world as well. For baptism makes us all Theotokoi! "Like Mary herself," a Roman Catholic homilist might well proclaim on this feast, "so we too in baptism have been 'conceived immaculately' in the watery womb of our baptismal mother." Surely the Solemnity of Mary's Assumption on August 15, by providing a concrete sign of our eschatological hope and future in Christ, for which baptism is itself the down payment by the gift of the Holy Spirit (see 2 Corinthians 1:21–22, Ephesians 1:13–14), might also suggest itself. And other sanctoral feasts, like the Nativity of St. John the Baptizer on June 24 or even other feasts of the Lord, like the Presentation on February 2, *forty days* after Christmas and already replete with baptismal images such as blessed candles (another name for this day is *Candlemas*), might, with some careful planning and imagination, be easily integrated into our baptismal consciousness and celebration.

Even with regard to multicultural issues in the contemporary church, significant feasts of particular cultural origins and importance might be looked at carefully in this regard. I am intrigued, for example, by the close theological parallels drawn by Virgilio Elizondo between Christmas, Easter and Pentecost and the apparition, narrative, image and continuing significance of the Virgin of Guadalupe, whose date of liturgical commemoration on December 12 has been recently raised in status from a memorial to a feast in all Roman Catholic dioceses of the Americas. Elizondo writes of the significance of the healing of Juan Diego's uncle, Juan Bernardino, in the Guadalupan narrative, saying:

> The restoration to life of the dying uncle on December 12 was nothing less than a historical resurrection of the dying peoples of the Americas who now came to life as the new Christian people of the Americas. Through Our Lady, a collective resurrection of the people would take place. The healing of Juan Bernardino constituted the assurance of survival through the new way of life of the Mother of Tepeyac. The people who had wanted only to die now began to want to live. This was the source of their dancing, feasting and joy. They were crucified [by the Spanish conquest] but not destroyed, crushed but not held down, for in her they were (and are) alive, risen and at the beginning of new life. Thus, liturgically, for us in the Americas, December 12 is as important a feast as December 25 and Easter Sunday are for the Christians of the Old World. . . . In the rehabilitation of Juan Bernardino, a totally new chapter in evangelization begins that will not be written about until our own times: evangelization by way of the incarnation. In the healing of Juan Bernardino, the conversion unto life of the people truly begins. In him begins the mestizo Christianity of the Americas.[33]

If it is indeed the case that the feast of the Virgin of Guadalupe is ultimately about a "new Pentecost," i.e., a resurrection and birthing of a new humanity in Christ by the Holy Spirit, a racially mixed or *mestizo* church of the Americas, then the parallels with baptism itself should be obvious. Elizondo himself relates the possible "Pentecost" character of this feast to the fact that within a few years of the date associated with the apparitions themselves the indigenous population of Mexico, like the three thousand converts in Acts 2:37–42, presented itself in great numbers (approximately eight million) for baptism.[34]

The multicultural, inclusive-catholic nature of the body of Christ, the incarnational face of the Communion of Saints, into which baptism incorporates us, is certainly reflected in the racially and culturally mixed face of the Virgin prophetically present on Juan Diego's *tilma*. While certainly this feast is of major importance for Mexican and Mexican-American Catholics, when it falls on an

Advent *Sunday* we would do well in our pursuit of further realizing that great baptismal vision of catholic wholeness and multiracial and multicultural inclusivity in Christ by paying close attention to the potential significance of this feast for the life of the church in general. Certainly in those communities where December 12 is celebrated fully, the rite of baptism itself could be integrated into the feast as a concrete sign of baptismal incorporation into this incarnational-ecclesiological reality of which the Virgin of Guadalupe serves as a most powerful icon.

In proposing the above baptismal approach to particular feasts, I am not suggesting that such feasts on the liturgical calendar are to be used or merely exploited in service to some baptismal "theme" being imposed upon them from the outside from a particular theological or pastoral agenda. Rather, I am suggesting that one of the hermeneutical keys to unlocking the very meaning of the feasts of the liturgical calendar themselves is *precisely* baptism. In other words, the *theme* of the liturgical year and every Sunday and feast, like the Paschal Mystery, *is* baptism. For the liturgical year itself is about catechesis and mystagogical understanding in the meaning of and the continual appropriation of our baptismal and ecclesiological identity as the body of Christ in the world.

Conclusion

As with the other baptismal images studied in this book, baptism as incorporation into the body of Christ also calls for our continued attention in our theological reflection and catechesis. Careful attention to the sacramental-incarnational being of the church as nothing less than Christ existing as church between his ascension and second coming helps us avoid the all too common cliché that liturgy is simply the "people's work" or "work of the   **131** people," a cliché increasingly being used to support all kinds of "liturgical" creations, especially within some "contemporary" worship forms becoming quite popular in various Protestant traditions.

While it is certainly true that liturgy is the people's work, liturgy is the work of this particular people which is Christ's body, and that body cannot be separated from its head. To use Augustine's phrase, liturgy is the work of the whole Christ, the *totus Christus,* both head and members, and it is that work precisely in its proclamation and sacramental-liturgical ritualizing. When that is understood correctly, then liturgy as the work of this people makes sense and even functions as a criterion for evaluating liturgical celebrations.

Similarly, renewed attention to our baptismal communion with Christ and the church suggests that attention also be given increasingly to the precise nature of the community of the church as a common priesthood and as an ecumenical, inclusive-catholic body, which finds its common identity in Christ the *one* high priest, who is not himself divided by ethnicity, gender or socio-economic status. At the same time, the very identity and nature of the church as the "Communion of Saints" suggests that the communion and community of the church be viewed, primarily, as a baptismal communion. And, as a way to underscore this reality, the Episcopal model of an All Saints' baptismal vigil either on or close to November 1, as well as the baptismal potential of other feasts on the liturgical calendar, including particular feasts from specific cultural contexts, is well worth our further theological and pastoral exploration and even experimentation.

As with the image of baptism as participation in the death, burial and resurrection of Christ, we have done quite well in general today with restoring an understanding of baptism as initiation or incorporation into the body of Christ. But we must be very clear on what the theological implications of that incorporation into

Christ actually are, both for baptism and for our understanding of the church itself. Together with what I have said in this chapter, certainly one way to underscore this notion of baptism as "entrance" into Christ and the church might still be the architectural placement of the baptismal font or pool near the literal entrance into the worship space of the liturgical assembly itself. The sign value for those who must pass by the font on the way into and on the way out of the worship space is a liturgical-baptismal value not to be neglected or ignored.

In recent years, however, even within some communities that have substantial fonts or pools at or near their entrances, there has been a tendency to ignore the font itself in favor of makeshift "fonts," often placed in the front of the liturgical assembly in order to enable the gathered assembly better to witness and, hence, participate more actively in the rite of baptism. While such attempts are certainly laudable, ignoring the font itself is a problematic development that should be curbed. If "seeing" is a great contemporary value, we should not forget that for centuries in the Roman Rite, baptism was customarily administered in baptistries apart from the assembly itself even *during* its public liturgies. In fact, one of the liturgical purposes of the Easter Vigil readings themselves was to occupy the attention of the liturgical assembly while baptisms were simultaneously taking place apart from the assembly. It was the entrance of the newly baptized into the assembly during the singing of the Litany of the Saints for the ratification, confirmation or sealing of baptism which followed that constituted the public participation of the assembly in this rite.

In those places where the baptismal space is not large enough to accommodate the presence of the entire assembly, then certainly some kind of adaptation of this tradition might be made, where, in the case of infants, the postbaptismal ("explanatory") rites of chrism, garment and candle or in the case of adults, especially within a

Roman Catholic context, confirmation might surely be celebrated after such a solemn entrance into the assembly has taken place. Here, again, words from Mark Searle remain most helpful:

> The consequences of believing that baptism should occur in the face of the whole congregation are . . . unfortunate. For one thing, it creates proscenium-style sanctuaries, where everything is enacted on-stage before a more or less passive audience and leads to a massive line-up of heavy symbols across the front of the church: font, paschal candle, lectern, altar, presider's chair, perhaps a second lectern for the cantor. It is essential, if we are to bring our ecclesial imaginations into line with the biblical ecclesiology of Vatican II, that we break that monopoly of symbols that reserves them all to an enclosed area "up front." Putting the font alongside or near the altar fosters clericalism, passive congregations and a voyeuristic experience of the most personal of all the sacraments. The radical personalism of this sacrament finds its supreme expression in the nakedness of the candidates, where they are reduced to the human condition in order to be raised to the divine. In centuries when Christians were more prudish than they are today, it must have taken a much more profound realization of the meaning of baptism than most of us possess to make such nudity even thinkable. But the same profound realization of the meaning of baptism that led to ritual nakedness also prompted the creation of baptistries, shaped as mausoleums or as martyr-shrines, where the mysteries hidden from outsiders and cherished by insiders, could take place with fitting decency. These baptistries would be visited by the baptized and venerated on the anniversary of their baptism, but they were never intended to accommodate more than the necessary few.[35]

Together with this, however, baptism as incorporation into the body of Christ calls unmistakably for the *public* celebration of baptism itself, whether in full view of the assembly or, depending upon available baptismal space, in a manner as suggested above. As the Roman Catholic General Introduction to Christian Initiation makes clear in the case of infants: "As far as possible, all recently born babies should be baptized at a common celebration on the same day."[36] And, as the Introduction to the *Rite of Baptism for Children* states:

> To bring out the paschal character of baptism, it is recommended that the sacrament be celebrated during the Easter Vigil or on Sunday, when the church commemorates the Lord's resurrection. On Sunday, baptism may be celebrated even during Mass, so that the entire community may be present and the relationship between baptism and eucharist may be clearly seen. . . . [37]

While the presence of parents, godparents, sponsors and other members of the church does certainly guarantee and signify that baptisms are never merely private but corporate-ecclesial sacramental events, the public celebration of baptism within the liturgical assembly is clearly a more fitting context which serves to underscore the importance of this image. As such, because baptism is incorporation into the body of Christ, the restoration of public baptism as a norm for Roman Catholic practice, as it already is (and has been for some time) in much of Protestantism, is certainly a goal worth pursuing. The image of baptism as incorporation into Christ and his body, the church, calls for such explicit liturgical concreteness and expression and anything we can do to make baptism an initiation more than a mere cliché about "community" should be considered seriously.

Chapter 5

Conclusion

■

This study has had in mind from the beginning the statement from the Roman Catholic General Introduction to *Christian Initiation,* where it is clearly stated that: "As far as possible, all recently born babies should be baptized at a common celebration on the same day."[1] Similarly, this study has attempted to take seriously the following directive in the Introduction to the Roman Catholic *Rite of Baptism for Children:*

> To bring out the paschal character of baptism, it is recommended that the sacrament be celebrated during the Easter Vigil or on Sunday, when the Church commemorates the Lord's resurrection. On Sunday, baptism may be celebrated even during Mass, so that the entire community may be present and the relationship between baptism and eucharist may be clearly seen; *but this should not be done too often.*[2]

One possible way, it seems, to ensure both "a common celebration on the same day" for "all recently born babies" at a "not too often" Sunday eucharistic celebration would be to schedule periodic Sunday or festival baptismal Masses at which recently born babies would be baptized together. A "Sunday" eucharistic celebration of baptism need not always be interpreted as one of the "regular" Sunday eucharists. Rather, just as special celebrations of first communion and confirmation in Roman Catholic practice tend to be scheduled at other times on Sundays and infant baptisms themselves tend to be celebrated in several places in a similar fashion, there is probably no reason why periodic "baptismal eucharists" could not be similarly planned.

This could easily be done, it appears to me, in close connection with a rediscovery of the numerous baptism-oriented feasts present throughout the liturgical year as I have underscored throughout this book. For good theo-logical reasons we may have centered our attention on the connection between Easter, especially the Easter Vigil, and Christian initiation. But as we have seen repeatedly, even if centered here today, the baptismal tradition of the church is much richer than this and, I believe, invites us to reconsider the overall contemporary dominance of Easter baptism. My graduate students know that I like to say, somewhat regretfully, that "we have tended to place all of our baptismal eggs in the Easter basket today." But surely, without minimizing the importance or sig-nificance of Easter baptism in the least, other occasions like Epiphany (or, more regularly, the Sunday after the Epiphany), where the baptism of Jesus is celebrated, Pentecost or All Saints suggest themselves as most fitting and suitable occasions for the celebration of baptism itself, just as other feasts of Mary and the saints might also be quite appropriate.

With these feasts as the four primary occasions for both baptismal vigils and the corporate and public (but not "too often") celebration of baptism throughout the liturgical year, parish catechetical programs (especially for the prebaptismal preparation of parents, godparents, and sponsors) might also be easily structured in the fall, winter and spring in close proximity to these festal occasions. In those places where the sheer number of infant baptismal candidates simply makes waiting for one of these major feasts problematic, certainly other feasts on the calendar suggest themselves as suitable baptismal occasions as well, with the result that in addition to these four central feasts, other regular occasions in relationship to the liturgical year might be highlighted. The words of Tertullian are still true in this context:

> The Passover [i.e., Easter] provides the day of most solemnity for baptism, for then was accomplished our Lord's passion, and *into it we are baptized*. . . . After that, Pentecost is a most auspicious period for arranging baptisms, for during it our Lord's resurrection was several times made known among the disciples, and the grace of the Holy Spirit first given. . . . For all that, every day is a Lord's day: any hour, any season, is suitable for baptism. If there is any difference of solemnity, it makes no difference to the grace.[3]

But if Tertullian was correct that "every day is a Lord's day: any hour, any season, is suitable for baptism," and that "if there is any difference of solemnity, it makes no difference to the grace," the fact remains that it is *precisely* this "difference of solemnity" associated with various feasts on the calendar that provides us with the very models of "grace" that baptism sacramentally signifies and effects. I remain convinced that baptism itself is one of the primary interpretative keys for understanding the meaning of the liturgical year itself, and it is from this conviction that this book has been written. Baptism, of course, is *always* participation in the death, burial and resurrection of Christ, and baptism *is* our common grave and tomb. But how better to underscore and highlight that than actual baptism at the Easter Vigil, after a Lent oriented toward baptismal-catechumenal preparation and/or renewal? Baptism, of course, is *always* new birth and adoption through water and the Holy Spirit. But how better to emphasize and bring this to light than by **139** the celebration of baptism on the feast of Jesus' own baptism, where our attention is directed to the divine declaration of Jesus' and our own baptismal identity conceived and given birth in the womb of the life-giving font, and where the Mothering Spirit descends to empower us for life and mission? Indeed, as we saw in chapter 2, attention to this might even help us come to celebrate the Advent season with new understanding and insight. Baptism, of course, is *always* the great sacrament and seal of the Holy Spirit. But how better to restore this much needed emphasis that Christian baptism is Spirit baptism than by celebrating baptism on Pentecost itself, where the Apostles themselves are "baptized" in the Holy Spirit and this "new birth" of the church is marked by the baptism of three thousand converts? And, baptism, of course, is *always* initiation or incorporation into Christ and his body, the church. But what better way to renew the ecclesiological dimension of baptism than to celebrate baptism on All Saints, when the very nature and communion of the church, both militant and triumphant, is already one of the major emphases in our liturgical celebration? Yes, Tertullian was correct in saying that "if there is any difference of solemnity, it makes no difference to the grace." Of course! But sacramental validity, or the "grace" of baptism, is not really the issue as we seek to do our baptismal catechesis and mystagogy in the best ways possible. Because the very "difference of solemnity" provides for us abundantly rich and various baptismal models and images for our celebration, understanding and lifelong appropriation of the meanings of baptism, we might say, instead, that the "difference of solemnity" makes all the difference.

The recovery of this "difference of solemnity" also may have vast ecumenical implications for the churches today as together we come to realize more fully what our common baptism signifies for our life together in Christ. In my article, "Let's Stop Making 'Converts' at Easter," I provided the following model for an ecumenical Easter Vigil with baptism that might be celebrated by Roman Catholics, Episcopalians, and Lutherans together:

> During this year's Easter Vigil, St. Mary's Roman Catholic Church, Our Savior's Lutheran Church and St. Alban's Episcopal Church, all located in Anywhere, celebrated most of the Easter Vigil together in one common place. Since St. Mary's was the host parish for this event, Fr. McCarthy presided over the blessing of the new fire and lighting of the Paschal Candle and offered the concluding prayers after each of the Vigil readings. An Episcopal deacon from St. Alban's carried the Paschal Candle in procession and intoned the Exsultet. Lectors came from all three parishes and a combined choir assisted with the appropriate responsorial psalms and other chants. Pastor Swanson from Our Savior's gave the Easter homily. At the time appointed for baptism and its renewal, an ecumenical "litany of the saints" was sung, the water was blessed by Father Smith from St. Alban's, who also led in the renunciation of Satan and the triple profession of faith. By turns, the "elect" from each parish (including infants) were baptized (including confirmation and/or the appropriate postbaptismal rites) by the respective ministers from those parishes in the presence of this common liturgical assembly. Following a common renewal of baptismal vows, a sprinkling rite and an exchange of peace, all three parish groups moved to two separate locations in the building for, unfortunately, two separate celebrations of the Eucharist [Episcopalians and Lutherans were together]. Yet, following those celebrations, all three assembled together again for a common concluding rite, the singing of a final hymn ("Jesus Christ Is Ris'n Today!" was chosen), and an Easter party in St. Mary's parish hall in honor of all those newly baptized that night in the *same* font. It is to such common and ecumenical origins in the baptismal waters that the forty days of Lent, the Paschal Triduum and the fifty days of Easter call us each year. Can we not commit ourselves anew to rid ourselves of any and everything that keeps us from this realization?[4]

In his recent book on liturgical ecclesiology, *Holy People,* Gordon Lathrop asks the following similar questions:

> If Baptism constitutes the assembly that is the church, ought not the Christians in a given locality enact that truth? Can

we not do much of the process of Baptism together? Could a renewed catechumenate be undertaken by many or even all of the Christian assemblies in a given local place? Could we be present at each other's baptisms? Could we do baptisms on the great feasts and do them side by side? Could we even consider constructing a single font for the local churches in our towns and cities?[5]

Such are the very questions that should arise for us when we take baptism in all its multifaceted imagery seriously for the continued life of the church.

It is my hope, then, that this study of only a few of these baptismal images might be of assistance to us in our ongoing task of plunging ourselves into the reality of what baptism has made us to be as we continue to live "after death" as newly born adopted children of God, sealed by the Holy Spirit dwelling in our hearts, within that *one* great Communion of Saints called church, on the way of our continual pilgrimage to the fullness of baptismal life in the reign of God.

Notes

Introduction

[1]*Procatechesis* 16. English translation from F. L. Cross, *St. Cyril of Jerusalem, Lectures on the Christian Sacraments* (Crestwood: St. Vladimir's Seminary Press, 1977), p. 50.

[2]Paul Bradshaw, *The Search for the Origins of Christian Worship* (London/New York: Oxford, 1992), pp. 46–47.

[3]RCIA, par. 222. See the very similar prayers in the *Lutheran Book of Worship* (Minneapolis: Augsburg Publishing House, 1978), p. 122; and the *Book of Common Prayer* (New York: Church Publishing, Inc., 1979), pp. 306–307.

[4]World Council of Churches, *Baptism, Eucharist, Ministry* (Geneva 1982), Baptism, II, pars. A–E.

[5]ibid., Baptism, II, par. 2.

[6]The first chapter of A. Dulles, *Models of the Church* (Garden City; Doubleday, 1974) still provides an excellent description of the use of models in theology.

[7]"One Body, One Spirit in Christ: The Eucharist as the Culmination of Christian Initiation," Annual Meeting of the Federation of Diocesan Liturgical Commissions, Minneapolis, Minnesota, October 10, 1996.

[8]*Book of Common Prayer* (New York: Church Hymnal Corporation, 1979), p. 312. *The Lutheran Book of Worship,* Minister's Edition (Minneapolis: Augsburg, 1978), p. 30, makes a similar statement.

[9]*Lutheran Book of Worship* (Minneapolis: Augsburg Publishing House, 1978), p. 121.

Chapter 1

[1]Tertullian, *De baptismo* 19, English translation from E. C. Whitaker, *Documents of the Baptismal Liturgy* (London: SPCK, 1970), p. 9 [emphasis added].

[2]Translation as quoted by Paul Bradshaw, " '*Diem baptismo sollemniorem*': Initiation and Easter in Christian Antiquity," in Maxwell Johnson (ed.), *Living Water, Sealing Spirit: Readings on Christian Initiation* (Collegeville: Pueblo, 1995), p. 138.

[3]See Thomas J. Talley, *The Origins of the Liturgical Year,* 2nd emended edition (Collegeville: Pueblo, 1986), pp. 18–27; and Paul F. Bradshaw, "The Origins of Easter," in P. Bradshaw and L. Hoffman (eds.), *Two Liturgical Traditions,* vol. 5: *Passover and Easter: Origin and History to Modern Times* (Notre Dame: University of Notre Dame Press, 1999), pp. 81–97. Unfortunately, the recent study by

Karl Gerlach, *The AnteNicene Pascha: A Rhetorical History,* Liturgia Condenda 7 (Louvain: Peeters, 1998), pp. 21–78, ignores recent scholarship on the question of baptism and Easter and assumes that baptism took place at the Quartodeciman Pasch as well.

4 See Raniero Cantalamessa, *Easter in the Early church* (Collegeville: The Liturgical Press, 1993), pp. 8–13.

5 See Paul Bradshaw, "Baptismal Practice in the Alexandrian Tradition: Eastern or Western?" in Maxwell Johnson (ed.), *Living Water, Sealing Spirit: Readings on Christian Initiation* (Collegeville: Pueblo, 1995), pp. 82–100.

6 For a summary of various theories as to how it was this came about see my recent study, *The Rites of Christian Initiation: Their Evolution and Interpretation* (Collegeville: Pueblo, 1999), pp. 106–112.

7 For texts of Augustine see Raniero Cantalamessa, *Easter in the Early church* (Collegeville: The Liturgical Press, 1993), pp. 108–115.

8 Paul F. Bradshaw, " '*Diem baptismo sollemniorem*': Initiation and Easter in Christian Antiquity," in Maxwell Johnson (ed.), *Living Water, Sealing Spirit: Readings on Christian Initiation* (Collegeville: Puelbo, 1995), p. 147.

9 Etty Hillesum, *An Interrupted Life,* as quoted in J. R. Baker, L. Nyberg, and V. Tufano (eds.), *A Baptism Sourcebook* (Chicago: Liturgy Training Publications, 1993), p. 49.

10 Joseph Sittler, "Aging: A Summing Up and a Letting Go," *Health and Medicine,* 2, 4, as quoted in

Virginia Sloyan (ed.), *Sourcebook About Christian Death* (Chicago: Liturgy Training Publications, 1990), p. 36.

11 Jennifer Glen, "Rites of Healings: A Reflection in Pastoral Theology," in Peter Fink (ed.), *Alternative Futures for Worship,* vol. 7: *Anointing of the Sick* (Collegeville: The Liturgical Press, 1987), as quoted in Virginia Sloyan (ed.), *Sourcebook about Christian Death* (Chicago: Liturgy Training Publications, 1990), pp. 32–33.

12 Jürgen Moltmann, *The Crucified God,* 2nd edition (New York: Harper & Row, Publishers, 1973), p. 40.

13 ibid., p. 33.

14 English translation from Edward Yarnold, *The Awe-Inspiring Rites of Initiation: The Origins of the R.C.I.A.,* 2nd edition (Collegeville: The Liturgical Press, 1994), pp. 77–78.

15 E. C. Whitaker, *Documents of the Baptismal Liturgy* (London: SPCK, 1970), pp. 31–32.

16 English translation is adapted from Yarnold, op. cit., pp. 155–56.

17 English translation is from Ibid., p. 119.

18 Whitaker, op. cit., p. 176.

19 ibid., p. 115.

20 ibid., pp. 125–26. [Emphasis is original].

21 Thomas Aquinas, *Summa Theologiae* 3a. 66, 7.2 in J. J. Cunningham (ed.), *St Thomas Aquinas, Summa Theologiae,* vol. 57: *Baptism and Confirmation (3a. 66–72)* (New York/London: McGraw Hill, 1975), p. 31. [Emphasis is original].

22 ibid., p. 32.

23 See Michel Dujarier, *A History of the Catechumenate* (New York: Sadlier, 1979), p. 133.

24 *Luther's Works,* vol. 26, pp. 67–68.

25 *Catechism of the Council of Trent for Parish Priests* (South Bend: Marian Publications, 1976), pp. 187–88.

26 *The Rites of the Catholic Church,* vol. 1 (Collegeville: Pueblo, 1990), par. 1, p. 3

27 *Catechism of the Catholic Church* (Collegeville: The Liturgical Press, 1994), par. 1227, p. 315.

28 RCIA, par. 222.

29 *Baptism, Eucharist, Ministry,* (Geneva: World Council of Churches, 1982), *Baptism,* par. 3.

30 Cf. *Welcome to Christ: Lutheran Rites for the Catechumenate* (Minneapolis: Augsburg Fortress, 1997).

31 *The Book of Occasional Services* (New York: Church Hymnal Corporation, 1979), pp. 112–127.

32 *Lutheran Book of Worship* (Minneapolis: Augsburg Publishing House, 1978), p. 121.

33 Jean Daniélou, "Le symbolisme des rites baptismaux," *Dieu vivant* 1 (1948) 17; English translation by Robert Taft, "Toward a Theology of Christian Feast," in idem, *Beyond East and West: Problems in Liturgical Understanding* (Washington, D.C.: The Pastoral Press, 1984), p. 11.

34 See his book by that title, *Life After Life: The Investigation of A Phenomenon—Survival of Bodily Death* (New York: Walker and Co., 1975), especially pp. 108–120. See also,

idem, *Reflections on Life After Life* (New York: Bantam Books, 1977). I owe these references to Mark Searle, who also treats this in various places in his writings.

35 Irene Nowell, "Biblical Images of Water," *Liturgy* (Summer 1987), as quoted in in J. R. Baker, L. Nyberg, and V. Tufano (eds.), *A Baptism Sourcebook* (Chicago: Liturgy Training Publications, 1993), p. 116.

36 T. Tappert (ed.), *The Book of Concord* (Philadelphia: Fortress Press, 1959), p. 349.

37 Martin Luther, *The Holy and Blessed Sacrament of Baptism, 1519,* in *Luther's Works,* vol. 35: *Word and Sacrament, I,* ed. E. Theodore Bachman (Philadelphia and Saint Louis: Fortress Press and Concordia Publishing House, 1960), pp. 30–31.

38 Mark Searle, "Editorial," *Assembly* 5:5 (March 1979), as printed in the worship folder for his Funeral Mass, August, 1992.

39 Joseph Cardinal Bernardin, *The Gift of Peace* (Chicago: Loyola Press, 1997), p. 136.

40 ibid., pp. 46–48.

41 ibid., p. 109.

42 Aidan Kavanagh, " Christian Initiation in Post-Conciliar Roman Catholicism: A Brief Report," in Maxwell Johnson (ed.), *Living Water, Sealing Spirit: Readings on Christian Initiation* (Collegeville: Pueblo, 1995), p. 10.

43 English translation in A. Flannery (ed.), *Vatican Council II: The Conciliar and Post Conciliar Documents,* vol. 1

(Collegeville: The Liturgical Press, 1984), p. 358.

44 *Ut Unum Sint* 6.

45 On the use of various models in ecclesiology see Avery Dulles, *Models of the Church,* Expanded Version (New York: Doubleday, Image, 1987).

46 Richard Cardinal Cushing, *The Servant Church* (Boston: Daughters of Saint Paul, 1966), pp. 6–8.

47 Dietrich Bonhoeffer, *The Cost of Discipleship,* unabridged edition (New York: The Macmillan Co., 1963), pp. 99, 101.

48 Dietrich Bonhoeffer, *Letters and Papers from Prison,* revised edition (New York: The Macmillan Co., 1967), pp. 203–204.

49 "The Church of Christ, in Every Age," *Lutheran Book of Worship* (Minneapolis: Augsburg Publishing House, 1978), Hymn 433.

Chapter 2

1 G. Austin, *The Rite of Confirmation: Anointing with the Spirit* (Collegeville 1985), p. 141.

2 Mark Searle, "Infant Baptism Reconsidered," in Maxwell Johnson (ed.), *Living Water, Sealing Spirit: Readings on Christian Initiation* (Collegeville: Pueblo, 1995), p. 385.

3 Kilian McDonnell, *The Baptism of Jesus in the Jordan: The Trinitarian and Cosmic Order of Salvation* (Collegeville: Michael Glazier, 1996), pp. 246–47.

4 Maxwell Johnson, *The Rites of Christian Initiation: Their Evolution and Interpretation* (Collegeville: Pueblo, 1999), pp. 381–82.

5 On this tradition see especially the work of G. Winkler, "The Original Meaning of the Prebaptismal Anointing and its Implications," in Maxwell Johnson (ed.), *Living Water, Sealing Spirit: Readings on Christian Initiation* (Collegeville: Pueblo, 1995), pp. 58–81; and the recent study of K. McDonnell, *The Baptism of Jesus in the Jordan: The Trinitarian and Cosmic Order of Salvation* (Collegeville: Michael Glazier, 1996).

6 Text adapted from E. C. Whitaker, *Documents of the Baptismal Liturgy* (London: SPCK, 1970), p. 12.

7 See ibid., pp. 16–17.

8 See Joseph Chalassery, *The Holy Spirit and Christian Initiation in the East Syrian Tradition,* Mar Thoma Yogam (Rome, 1995), pp. 46–47.

9 On this see Thomas Talley, *The Origins of the Liturgical Year,* Second Emended Edition, (Collegeville: Pueblo, 1986), pp. 163ff.

10 On Origen's baptismal theology see J. Laporte, "Models from Philo in Origen's Teaching on Original Sin," in Maxwell Johnson (ed.), *Living Water, Sealing Spirit,* op. cit., pp. 101–117; C. Blanc, "Le Baptême d'après Origène," *Studia Patristica* 11 (1972), pp. 113–124; H. Crouzel, "Origène et la structure du sacrement," in *Bulletin de littérature ecclesiastique* 2 (1962), pp. 81–92; J. Daniélou, *Bible and Liturgy* (Notre Dame: Univesity of Notre Dame Press, 1956), pp. 99–113; and idem, *Origen* (New York, 1955), pp. 52–61.

11 Text from G. Cuming, *Hippolytus: A Text for Students,* Grove Liturgical Study 8 (Bramcote/Nottingham 1976), p. 20.

12 Whitaker, op. cit., pp. 153–54 [all emphases are added].

13 ibid., pp. 154–58 [all emphases are added].

14 L. Deiss, *Springtime of the Liturgy* (Collegeville: The Liturgical Press, 1979), pp. 264–65 [all emphases are added].

15 Whitaker, op. cit., pp. 166–96 [all emphases are added].

16 Cyprian, *Ad Quirinium* 3.25.

17 Whitaker, op.cit., p. 107 [emphasis added].

18 Augustine, *De bapt.* 4.24.32 [emphasis added].

19 Augustine, *Ep.* 98.2 [emphasis added].

20 Whitaker, op.cit., pp. 127–33 [emphasis added].

21 ibid., pp. 138–47 [emphasis added].

22 Texts are cited from G. Jeanes, *The Day Has Come! Easter and Baptism in Zeno of Verona*, Alcuin Club Collections 73 (Collegeville 1995), pp. 97–98 [emphasis added].

23 ibid., pp. 79–80 [emphasis added].

24 ibid., p. 97 [emphasis added].

25 ibid., p. 68 [emphasis added].

26 Whitaker, op. cit., pp. 160–62.

27 ibid., pp. 208–212.

28 Whitaker, op. cit. p. 176.

29 See Gabriele Winkler, "Confirmation or Chrismation? A Study in Comparative Liturgy," and Joseph Levesque, "The Theology of the Postbaptismal Rites in the Seventh and Eighth Century Gallican Church," both in Maxwell Johnson (ed.), *Living Water, Sealing Spirit: Readings on Christian Initiation* (Collegeville: Pueblo, 1995), pp. 202–18 and 159–201.

30 Martin Luther, *The Order of Baptism, 1523,* in *Luther's Works,* vol. 51, p. 97 [emphasis added].

31 M. Luther, *The Order of Baptism Newly Revised, 1526,* in *Luther's Works,* vol. 51, p. 109 [emphasis added].

32 J. D. C. Fisher, *Christian Initiation: The Reformation Period* (London: SPCK, 1970), pp. 36–37 [emphasis added].

33 ibid., p. 89 [emphasis added].

34 ibid., p. 94 [emphasis added].

35 *Catechism of the Council of Trent for Parish Priests* (South Bend: Marian Publications, 1976), p. 163.

36 See A. Kavanagh, *Confirmation: Origins and Reform* (Collegeville 1988), p. 93.

37 *Lutheran Worship* (St. Louis: Concordia Publishing House, 1982), p. 203.

38 See Paul Bradshaw, "*Diem baptismo sollemniorem:* Baptism and Easter in Christian Antiquity," reprinted in Maxwell Johnson (ed.), *Living Water, Sealing Spirit: Readings on Christian Initiation,* op. cit., pp. 137–47.

39 G. Jeanes, *The Day Has Come! Easter and Baptism in Zeno of Verona,* op. cit., pp. 256–57 [emphasis added].

40 RCIA, par. 222 [emphasis added].

41 Dominic Serra, "The Blessing of Baptismal Water at the Paschal Vigil:

Ancient Texts and Modern Revisions," *Worship* (1990), pp. 153–55. See also idem., "The Blessing of Baptismal Water at the Paschal Vigil in the *Gelasianum Vetus:* A Study of the Euchological Texts, Ge 444–48," *Ecclesia Orans 6* (1989): 323–44.

42 *Rite of Baptism for Children,* paragraph 54.

43 ibid., paragraph 62.

44 ibid., paragraph 63.

45 Cf. Joseph Challassery, *The Holy Spirit and Christian Initiation in the East Syrian Tradition* (Mar Thoma Yogam, Rome 1995).

46 I am basing this comment on a slide presentation of early baptismal fonts in North Africa presented by Dr. Robin M. Jensen at the annual meeting of the North American Patristics Society, Loyola University, Chicago, Illinois, in June 1994. See Jensen's forthcoming book on baptismal art and architecture, and see also Regina Kuehn's study of baptismal fonts, *A Place for Baptism* (Chicago: Liturgy Training Publications, 1992).

47 Athanasius, *De Incarnatione Verbi Dei,* 54.

48 *Sermo 1 in Nativitate Domini;* English translation from The Liturgy of the Hours, vol. 1 (New York 1975), p. 405.

49 *The Book of Occasional Services* (New York: Church Hymnal Corporation, 1979), pp. 49–50.

50 See Paul Bradshaw, "*Diem baptismo sollemniorem:* Initiation and Easter in Christian Antiquity," in Maxwell E. Johnson (ed.), *Living Water, Sealing Spirit: Readings on Christian Initia-*

tion (Collegeville: Pueblo, 1995), pp. 143–145.

51 See L. C. Mohlberg (ed.), *Missale Gothicum* (Rome: Herder, 1961), pp. 20–24.

52 See Thomas Talley, The Origins of the Liturgical Year, 2nd emended edition (Collegeville: Pueblo, 1986), pp. 147ff.; and J. Neil Alexander, *Waiting for the Coming: The Meaning of Advent, Christmas, and Epiphany* (Washington, D.C.: The Pastoral Press, 1993), pp. 8–23.

53 See Martin Connell, "The Origins and Evolution of Advent in the West," in Maxwell E. Johnson (ed.), *Between Memory and Hope: Readings on the Liturgical Year* (Collegeville: The Liturgical Press, 2000).

54 *The Book of Occasional Services* (New York: Church Hymnal Corporation, 1979), pp. 120, 124.

55 See *Living Witnesses: The Adult Catechumenate: Congregational Prayers to Accompany the Catechumenal Process* (Winnipeg: The Evangelical Lutheran Church in Canada, 1992), pp. 7, 17, 21–22, and 26. Unfortunately, the recent version of the process, *Welcome to Christ: Lutheran Rites for the Catechumenate* (Minneapolis: Augsburg Fortress, 1997), prepared jointly by the Evangelical Lutheran Church in America and the Lutheran Church–Missouri Synod, gives far less attention to Epiphany as a baptismal occasion than does its Canadian Lutheran counterpart.

56 Raymond Brown, *An Adult Christ at Christmas* (Collegeville: The Liturgical Press, 1978).

57 *Rite of Dedication of a Church,* 62.

[58] Regina Kuehn, *A Place for Baptism* (Chicago: Liturgy Training Publications, 1992). p. 3.

[59] Kilian McDonnell, *The Baptism of Jesus* (Collegeville: Michael Glazier, 1996), pp. 231–32.

[60] Mark Searle, "Infant Baptism Reconsidered," in Maxwell E. Johnson (ed.), *Living Water, Sealing Spirit: Readings on Christian Initiation* (Collegeville: Pueblo, 1995), p. 391.

[61] ibid., pp. 385–86.

[62] See P. Bradshaw, *The Search for the Origins of Christian Worship* (New York/London 1992), pp. 59–60, 63–65.

Chapter 3

[1] Peter Cramer, *Baptism & Change in the Early Middle Ages, circa 200–1150,* Cambridge Studies in Medieval Life and Thought, Fourth Series, vol. 20 (Cambridge 1993) p. 137.

[2] *The Rites of the Catholic Church,* vol. 1, op. cit., pp. 146–47.

[3] See Kilian McDonnell and and G. T. Montague, *Christian Initiation and Baptism in the Holy Spirit: Evidence from the First Eight Centuries* (Collegeville.The Liturgical Press, 1991), pp. 31-39; and G. Austin, *Anointing,* op. cit., pp. 7–9.

[4] *General Introduction to Christian Initiation,* par. 3, 4 and 5.

[5] World Council of Churches, *Baptism, Eucharist, Ministry* (Geneva 1982), par. 5.

[6] *Rite of Baptism for Children,* par. 49 [emphasis added].

[7] ibid., par. 54.

[8] RCIA, paragraphs 233–235.

[9] *The Book of Common Prayer* (New York: Church Hymnal Corporation, 1979), p. 308.

[10] *Lutheran Book of Worship,* Minister's Edition (Minneapolis: Augsburg, 1978), p. 311.

[11] Paul Turner, *Confirmation: The Baby in Solomon's Court* (Mahwah:Paulist Press, 1993), p. 129.

[12] On this point, see my recent essay, "Let's Stop Making 'Converts' at Easter," *Catechumenate* 21, 5 (September 1999), pp. 10–20.

[13] RCIA, par. 1 [emphasis added].

[14] World Council of Churches, *Baptism, Eucharist and Ministry* (Geneva 1982), par. 5.

[15] *Joint Declaration,* par. 15 and 16 [emphasis added].

[16] ibid., par. 18.

[17] ibid., par. 25 [emphasis added].

[18] Eugene Brand, *Baptism: A Pastoral Perspective* (Minneapolis: Augsburg, 1975), p. 38.

[19] *The Sacramentary of the Roman Missal* (Collegeville: The Liturgical Press, 1985), pp. 510–11.

[20] ibid., pp. 513–14.

[21] ibid., pp. 518, 520.

[22] ibid., pp. 1142, 1144.

[23] ibid., pp. 1146–48.

[24] *Eucharistic Prayer for Masses for Various Needs and Occasions* (Collegeville: The Liturgical Press, 1994), pp. 16, 19.

25 *Book of Common Prayer,* op. cit., p. 363.

26 ibid., p. 369.

27 ibid., p. 375.

28 *Lutheran Book of Worship,* Ministers' Edition, op. cit., p. 223.

29 ibid., p. 225.

30 ibid., p. 226.

31 *Catechism of the Catholic Church* (Collegeville: The Liturgical Press, 1994), par. 1358, p. 342.

32 ibid., par. 1375, p. 346.

33 Aidan Kavanagh, *Confirmation: Origins and Reform* (Collegeville: Pueblo, 1988), p. 50.

34 English translation adapted from Geoffrey Cuming, *Hippolytus,* op. cit., p. 11.

35 Tertullian, *De baptismo* 19, English translation from E. C. Whitaker, op. cit., p. 9 [emphasis added].

36 Standard theories on the development of Pentecost are provided by Robert Cabié, *La Pentecôte: L'évolution de la Cinquantaine pascale au cours des cinq premiers siècles* (Tournai 1964), and Patrick Regan, "The Fifty Days and the Fiftieth Day," *Worship* 55 (1981), pp. 194–218 (found in Maxwell E. Johnson (ed.), *Between Memory and Hope: Readings on the Liturgical Year* [Collegeville: The Liturgical Press, 2000]).

37 On this, see Paul Bradshaw, " '*Diem baptismo sollemniorem:'* Initiation and Easter in Christian Antiquity," in Maxwell Johnson, *Living Water, Sealing Spirit,* op. cit., p. 144.

38 See Walter Ray, *August 15 and the Development of the Jerusalem Calendar* (PhD. Dissertation, University of Notre Dame, 2000), pp. 275–77.

39 *Book of Occasional Services* (New York: Church Hymnal Corporation, 1979), pp. 126–27.

40 Congregation for Divine Worship, *Concerning the Preparation and Celebration of the Easter Feasts* (January 16, 1988), no. 107.

41 Frederick Dale Bruner and William Hordern, *The Holy Spirit— Shy Member of the Trinity* (Minneapolis: Augsburg, 1984).

42 Regin Prenter, *Spiritus Creator* (Philadelphia: Fortress, 1953), pp. 52–53.

43 ibid., pp. 53–54.

Chapter 4

1 See *Lumen Gentium* 1.

2 See Edward Schillebeeckx, *Christ the Sacrament of the Encounter with God* (New York: Sheed and Ward, 1963).

3 See Karl Rahner, *The Church and the Sacraments* (London: Burns & Oates), 1963.

4 Dietrich Bonhoeffer, *Christ the Center* (New York: Harper & Row, 1960), pp. 59-60.

5 Carl Braaten, *Mother Church: Ecclesiology and Ecumenism* (Minneapolis: Fortress Press, 1998), p. 7 [emphasis added]. See also the recent work on ecclesiology by Gordon Lathrop, *Holy People: A Liturgical Ecclesiology* (Minneapolis: Fortress, 1999).

6 Avery Dulles, *Models of the church,* expanded edition (New York: Doubleday, Image, 1987), p. 61.

[7] James Dallen, "Liturgy and Justice for All," *Worship* 65, 4 (1991), p. 302.

[8] Kenneth Himes, "Eucharist and Justice: Assessing the Legacy of Virgil Michel," *Worship* 63, 3 (1988), pp. 220–21.

[9] Nathan *Mitchell, Eucharist as Sacrament of Initiation,* Forum Essays, Number 2 (Chicago: Liturgy Training Publications, 1994), pp. 130–32.

[10] Dallen, op. cit., p. 306.

[11] Dietrich Bonhoeffer, *Life Together: A Discussion of Christian Fellowship* (New York: Harper & Row, 1954), p. 30.

[12] ibid., p. 39.

[13] *The Rites of the Catholic Church,* vol. 1 (Collegeville: Pueblo, 1990), #319, p. 208.

[14] *Lutheran Book of Worship* (Minneapolis: Augsburg, 1978), p. 124.

[15] *Catechism of the Catholic Church* (Collegeville: The Liturgical Press, 1994), #1268, p. 323 [emphasis is original].

[16] Aidan Kavanagh, "Unfinished and Unbegun Revisited," in Maxwell Johnson (ed.), *Living Water, Sealing Spirit* (Collegeville: Pueblo, 1995), pp. 267–69.

[17] ibid., pp. 270–71.

[18] World Council of Churches, "Baptism," par. D.6, *Baptism, Eucharist, Ministry* (Geneva, 1982).

[19] *Catechism of the Catholic Church* (Collegeville: The Liturgical Press, 1994), #1271, p. 323 [emphasis is original].

[20] Maxwell Johnson, *The Rites of Christian Initiation: Their Evolution and Interpretation* (Collegeville: Pueblo, 1999), pp. 367–68.

[21] Nathan Mitchell, *Eucharist as Sacrament of Initiation,* Forum Essays, Number 2 (Chicago: Liturgy Training Publications, 1994), pp. 130-31.

[22] H. George Anderson, J. Francis Stafford and Joseph A. Burgess (eds.), *The One Mediator, the Saints and Mary,* Lutherans and Catholics in Dialogue VIII (Minneapolis: Augsburg, 1992), p. 117.

[23] See the essay by James White, "Forgetting and Remembering the Saints," Liturgy 14, 3 (Winter 1998), pp. 27–39, for a summary both of historical attitudes toward the saints in Protestantism and for the recovery of the sanctoral cycle today.

[24] *Lutheran Book of Worship* (Minneapolis: Augsburg, 1978), pp. 10–12. Hardly a day is left without a commemoration of someone.

[25] ibid., pp. 36–38.

[26] *Lutheran Book of Worship,* Minister's Edition (Minneapolis: Augsburg, 1978), p. 256 [emphasis added].

[27] *Welcome to Christ: Lutheran Rites for the Catechumenate* (Minneapolis: Augsburg, 1997), pp. 70–71.

[28] *Lutheran Book of Worship,* Minister's Edition (Minneapolis: Augsburg, 1978), p. 189.

[29] *Apology of the Augsburg Confession,* Art. XXI, in Theodore Tappert (ed.), *The Book of Concord* (Philadelphia: Fortress, 1959), pp. 229–30).

[30] "The Church's One Foundation," stanza 5, *Lutheran Book of Worship* (Minneapolis: Augsburg, 1978), Hymn 369.

31 *The Book of Common Prayer* (New York: Church Hymnal Corporation, 1979), p. 245 [emphasis added]. The opening prayer in *Lutheran Book of Worship* for the festival of All Saints is a variation of this Episcopal prayer.

32 *The Book of Occasional Services* (New York: The Church Hymnal Corporation, 1979), pp. 104–105.

33 Virgil Elizondo, *Guadalupe: Mother of the New Creation* (Maryknoll, New York: Orbis Books, 1997), p. 93.

34 See Virgilio Elizondo and Timothy Matovina, *Mestizo Worship: A Pastoral Approach to Liturgical Ministry* (Collegeville: The Liturgical Press, 1998), pp. 21, 28–29.

35 Mark Searle, "Foreword," in Regina Kuehn, *A Place for Baptism* (Chicago: Liturgy Training Publications, 1992), p. v.

36 *The Rites of the Catholic Church,* vol. 1 (Collegeville: Pueblo, 1990), p. 10.

37 ibid., p. 369.

Chapter 5

1 *Rites,* vol. 1, p. 10.

2 ibid., p. 369 [Emphasis added].

3 Tertullian, *De baptismo* 19, English translation from E. C. Whitaker, *Documents of the Baptismal Liturgy* (London: SPCK, 1970), p. 9 [emphasis added].

4 Maxwell E. Johnson, "Let's Stop Making 'Converts' at Easter," *Catechumenate* 21, 5 (1999), pp. 18–19.

5 Gordon Lathrop, *Holy People: A Liturgical Ecclesiology* (Minneapolis: Fortress, 1999), pp. 146–47.